D1265316

DISEASES & DISORDERS

Diabetes

Titles in the Diseases and Disorders series include:

Acne
AIDS
Alcoholism
Allergies
Alzheimer's Disease
Amnesia
Anorexia and Bulimia
Anthrax
Anxiety Disorders
Arthritis
Asperger's Syndrome
Asthma
Attention Deficit Disorder
Autism
Bipolar Disorder
Birth Defects
Blindness
Brain Trauma
Brain Tumors
Breast Cancer
Cancer
Cerebral Palsy
Childhood Obesity
Chronic Fatigue
    Syndrome
Deafness
Dementia
Diabetes
Dyslexia
The Ebola Virus
Epilepsy
Flu
Food Poisoning
Growth Disorders
Headaches
Heart Disease
Hepatitis

Hodgkins Disease
Human Papilloma Virus (HPV)
Infectious Mononucleosis
Leukemia
Lou Gehrig's Disease
Lung Cancer
Lupus
Lyme Disease
Malaria
Malnutrition
Measles and Rubella
Meningitis
Mood Disorders
Muscular Dystrophy
Obesity
Obsessive Compulsive
    Disorder
Ovarian Cancer
Parkinson's Disease
Phobias
Postpartum Depression
Post-Traumatic Stress
    Disorder
Prostate Cancer
SARS
Sexually Transmitted
    Diseases
Sickle Cell Anemia
Skin Cancer
Smallpox
Strokes
Sudden Infant Death
    Syndrome
Teen Depression
Toxic Shock Syndrome
Tuberculosis
West Nile Virus

DISEASES &
DISORDERS

Diabetes

Barbara Stahura

LUCENT BOOKS

A part of Gale, Cengage Learning

GALE
CENGAGE Learning

Detroit • New York • San Francisco • New Haven, Conn • Waterville, Maine • London

© 2009 Gale, Cengage Learning

LIBRARY OF CONGRESS CATALOGING-IN-PUBLICATION DATA

Stahura, Barbara.
  Diabetes / by Barbara Stahura.
    p. cm. — (Diseases & disorders)
  Includes bibliographical references and index.
  ISBN 978-1-4205-0114-8 (hardcover)
  1. Diabetes. I. Title.
  RC660.5.S73 2009
  616.4'62—dc22

                                                    2008043984

Lucent Books
27500 Drake Rd.
Farmington Hills, MI 48331

ISBN-13: 978-1-4205-0114-8
ISBN-10: 1-4205-0114-3

Printed in the United States of America
1 2 3 4 5 6 7 13 12 11 10 09

Table of Contents

"The Most Difficult Puzzles Ever Devised"

Charles Best, one of the pioneers in the search for a cure for diabetes, once explained what it is about medical research that intrigued him so. "It's not just the gratification of knowing one is helping people," he confided, "although that probably is a more heroic and selfless motivation. Those feelings may enter in, but truly, what I find best is the feeling of going toe to toe with nature, of trying to solve the most difficult puzzles ever devised. The answers are there somewhere, those keys that will solve the puzzle and make the patient well. But how will those keys be found?"

Since the dawn of civilization, nothing has so puzzled people— and often frightened them, as well—as the onset of illness in a body or mind that had seemed healthy before. A seizure, the inability of a heart to pump, the sudden deterioration of muscle tone in a small child—being unable to reverse such conditions or even to understand why they occur was unspeakably frustrating to healers. Even before there were names for such conditions, even before they were understood at all, each was a reminder of how complex the human body was, and how vulnerable.

While our grappling with understanding diseases has been frustrating at times, it has also provided some of humankind's most heroic accomplishments. Alexander Fleming's accidental discovery in 1928 of a mold that could be turned into penicillin has resulted in the saving of untold millions of lives. The isolation of the enzyme insulin has reversed what was once a death sentence for anyone with diabetes. There have been great strides in combating conditions for which there is not yet a cure, too. Medicines can help AIDS patients live longer, diagnostic tools such as mammography and ultrasounds can help doctors find tumors while they are treatable, and laser surgery techniques have made the most intricate, minute operations routine.

This "toe-to-toe" competition with diseases and disorders is even more remarkable when seen in a historical continuum. An astonishing amount of progress has been made in a very short time. Just two hundred years ago, the existence of germs as a cause of some diseases was unknown. In fact, it was less than 150 years ago that a British surgeon named Joseph Lister had difficulty persuading his fellow doctors that washing their hands before delivering a baby might increase the chances of a healthy delivery (especially if they had just attended to a diseased patient)!

Each book in Lucent's Diseases and Disorders series explores a disease or disorder and the knowledge that has been accumulated (or discarded) by doctors through the years. Each book also examines the tools used for pinpointing a diagnosis, as well as the various means that are used to treat or cure a disease. Finally, new ideas are presented—techniques or medicines that may be on the horizon.

Frustration and disappointment are still part of medicine, for not every disease or condition can be cured or prevented. But the limitations of knowledge are being pushed outward constantly; the "most difficult puzzles ever devised" are finding challengers every day.

The Sugar Disease

In the twenty-first century, amazing technology is helping doctors diagnose diseases. From genetic testing to scanning machines, technology lets doctors and technicians look inside the body in ways not possible only a few decades ago. For many centuries, however, doctors had to depend on their knowledge of the human body (which was extremely limited compared with today's knowledge) and their powers of observation.

Even thousands of years ago, doctors observed that some of their patients were always hungry and ate large amounts of food but still grew very thin, as though they were starving. They often felt weak and sleepy and even fell unconscious. Most important, they suffered from a horrible thirst that no amount of liquid could quench, and they had to urinate *a lot*— sometimes 10 or more quarts (9.64 liters) a day. In today's world, that amount would fill nearly five two-liter soda bottles.

Furthermore, doctors noticed that the urine of these patients smelled extremely sweet. Doctors in ancient India called it "honey urine" and saw "the attraction of flies and ants to the urine of those affected by this ailment."[1] In seventeenth-century Europe, doctors tasted the urine of these patients and found it to be sugary. So, this illness came to be known as the Sugar Disease. Sadly, people with Sugar Disease died quickly because no treatment or cure for this mysterious illness existed.

We now call this illness diabetes mellitus, or simply diabetes. Although it is a very serious, potentially deadly disease, people who have it can live long, productive lives if they take good care of themselves. Thomas Edison, the creator of the lightbulb and many other inventions, had diabetes and lived to age eighty-four. Laura Ingalls Wilder, who wrote the "Little House" books, lived until age ninety despite her diabetes. Many famous people today live well with this disease. Among them are actress Halle Berry and singers Nick Jonas of the Jonas Brothers and Elliot Yamin from *American Idol*. Even top athletes have diabetes, including Olympic swimmer Gary Hall, Chris Dudley of the New York Knicks, and Billie Jean King of tennis fame.

Actress Halle Berry is one of many celebrities that live with diabetes.

However, even though diabetes can now be managed, having the disease is not so sweet. The Centers for Disease Control and Prevention says, "Overall, the risk for death among people with diabetes is about twice that of people without diabetes of similar age."[2] People with diabetes often die from heart disease, and they have a two to four times greater risk of stroke. Nearly three-fourths of adults with diabetes have high blood pressure or take drugs to control high blood pressure. Kidney failure, blindness, and blood circulation problems in the toes, feet, and legs (which can require amputation) are also common complications, particularly in people who are not able to control their diabetes well.

Good News About Diabetes

Fortunately, modern medicine has brought hope to many diabetics, or people with diabetes. Unlike in centuries past, the cause of diabetes is now well known, and many medicines and other treatments can help diabetics control their illness. Some diabetics must take insulin several times a day, but others do not. Diabetics must be careful with their nutrition and watch their weight, monitor their blood sugar frequently, and stay active, but they can often live energetic, productive lives as well.

Two people who have lived a very long time after being diagnosed with diabetes in childhood are Robert and Gerald Cleveland, brothers who live in Syracuse, New York. They developed diabetes shortly after the discovery of insulin in 1921, and more than seven decades later, neither one of them has developed any serious complications.

They say their mother, Henrietta, carefully taught them how to care for themselves so they could stay healthy. "The doctor prescribed the diet I should be on, and my mother was most careful about sticking to it," Robert Cleveland says. "There were very few carbohydrates, a quart and a half of milk every day, and there were lots of vegetables and proteins."[3]

Another remarkable diabetes success story is Gladys Dull. She has been taking insulin since 1924, just a few months before she turned seven. Gladys is believed to be the oldest living person with diabetes, and she is still going strong in her nineties, thanks in large part to never missing an insulin shot. She calculates she has had more than sixty thousand shots since 1924. Furthermore, this lively ninety-year-old says she has survived so well and so long with diabetes because she remained active most of her life and has always eaten a healthy diet. "When I was younger, I did everything—horseback riding, cycling, snowmobiling, motorcycle riding—I always stayed active,"[4] she says. In addition, Gladys still very carefully determines her portions of food and has remained on a similar diet her whole life, which means her insulin requirements do not change much. "I give my mother credit for that," she says. "She was strict with me, and I thank her for it now."[5]

The Cleveland brothers and Gladys Dull have done an excellent job of controlling their diabetes, even though for much of their lives they did not have the gifts of the medical technology and drugs we have today. This shows that with proper care, the battle with diabetes can be won through daily hard work. Today, research into this illness continues, and people who are diagnosed with diabetes have a better-than-ever chance of surviving, and surviving well, for many years.

CHAPTER ONE

What Is Diabetes?

While diabetes has long been part of human life, its frequency has rocketed upward in recent years. In the last two decades, the number of people with diabetes around the world has risen from 30 million to 230 million. That number is expected to keep climbing and reach 350 million by 2025. The World Health Organization has declared diabetes the health hazard for the twenty-first century.

The situation is no different in the United States, where this disease is now the seventh leading cause of death. From 1997 to 2003, the numbers of Americans diagnosed with diabetes rose by an astounding 41 percent. By 2007, 8 percent of all the people in this country—24 million—had diabetes. More than 6 million of those people do not realize they have the disease, which puts them at great risk. Researchers say the diabetes epidemic will continue to grow worse, since more than 57 million additional Americans have a condition called prediabetes, or high blood sugar not yet at diabetic levels. These people have a high likelihood of developing full-blown diabetes.

This epidemic is creating serious problems for children. In the past, diabetes of any kind was uncommon in kids. Today, however, tens of thousands of young Americans have diabetes, and "of all babies born [in America] in 2000, one-third will become diabetic sometime in their lives unless they begin eating a lot better and getting a lot more exercise,"[6] according to the Centers for Disease Control and Prevention.

Reasons for the Diabetes Epidemic

The reason so many children and adults now live with diabetes or face its threat in the future is because of another epidemic now under way in the United States: being seriously over-weight. By far the largest cause for the alarming upswing in the number of diabetes cases is the upsurge of obesity that has hit adults and children alike in the United States. Obesity is the "fastest-growing cause of disease and death in America today,"[7] according to Richard Carmona, the former surgeon general of the United States.

Nearly two out of three Americans are overweight or obese, and more than 15 percent of young Americans aged six to seventeen fall into that category—more than 8 million. Many of them will develop diabetes, since obese children are twice as likely to develop the disease than those of normal weight. Obesity increases the chances of developing at least one form of diabetes. That form of diabetes is called type 2 diabetes. Too much fat, especially around the waist and abdomen, harms the process by which muscles can absorb glucose. And since diabetes occurs when glucose absorption is poor or nonexistent, being fat can contribute to the development of diabetes.

"A direct result of the obesity epidemic is that type 2 diabetes, previously unheard of in young people, is trickling into our schools," Carmona said. "And if left unchecked, it leads to serious illness and possible death."[8]

Fortunately, though, type 2 diabetes can often be prevented by a lifestyle that includes eating a healthy diet and getting enough activity. Furthermore, once someone has developed type 2, it can often be well controlled that same way.

But neither of these epidemics will disappear quickly. According to Carmona, "This effort is probably going to be intergenerational because we have a society of 200 million people who need to change their purchasing patterns, their eating patterns, activity patterns. It will take a while. If we start today, hopefully

The rise in obesity among adults and children in the United States, fueled by poor diets and inactive lifestyles, has caused the number of diabetes cases to increase dramatically.

we build a legacy, the children inherit it, and it gets better as the generations go along, because we didn't get here overnight. It's taken us decades."[9]

How Diabetes Happens

Diabetes is a chronic illness, which means it lasts a long time, perhaps for life. It is not contagious. Diabetes occurs because the body cannot properly use the sugar that comes from food. The body gets most of its quick energy from a kind of sugar called glucose, and it pulls glucose out of food during digestion. The process of digestion breaks down food into very, very small parts that can be absorbed by the bloodstream. Diabetes results when something happens to disrupt part of this process.

When a person begins eating, digestion also begins. Saliva starts the complex process of breaking down that bite of chicken or bread or apple even before it leaves the mouth. Swallowing food sends it down the esophagus and delivers it to the stomach, where strong natural acids called gastric juices continue breaking down the food into smaller and smaller pieces.

The intestines are next in line in the digestion process. An average adult human intestine can be more than 30 feet (9m) long, divided into the small and large intestines. Food traveling all that way has plenty of time to break down into the tiniest, most basic forms our bodies can use, including molecules of proteins, carbohydrates, fats, and vitamins. One important kind of carbohydrate is the sugar called glucose, which keeps muscles moving and creates important chemical reactions in the body by providing instant energy.

Glucose is also the only energy source for the brain. It is absorbed through the intestinal walls into the bloodstream, and then it travels to every part of the body.

The pancreas is a flat gland located behind the stomach. It is about the size of a hand. Inside the pancreas are thousands of cell clusters called islets of Langerhans, and they contain a special kind of cell called beta cells. The beta cells create insulin, which is a hormone that combines with glucose to help glucose move into all the trillions of cells in the body and give them energy so they can do their jobs well. A healthy pancreas produces just the right amount of insulin around the clock, based on the amount of glucose circulating in the bloodstream. (This glucose in the bloodstream is also called blood sugar.)

However, if the pancreas cannot make insulin, or if the body cannot use the insulin it produces, the glucose cannot get into the cells. It stays in the bloodstream, keeping the blood sugar levels high and causing damage to the organs in the body. For instance, the eyes of a diabetic person can be damaged by high blood sugars causing blockages in the tiny blood vessels or preventing enough oxygen from reaching the eyes. This can lead to blindness. Diabetes can also cause the kidneys to fail, and then they cannot properly eliminate waste products from the body, which leads to death. Diabetes harms the nervous system by causing a condition called neuropathy. When neuropathy affects the nerves in the feet or legs, they become numb. This can lead to serious foot infections and even amputation of the feet or legs.

Four types of diabetes affect millions of Americans as well as millions of other people around the world. They are type 2, type 1, type 1.5, and gestational. By far, the most common is type 2.

Type 2 Diabetes

About 75 percent of people with diabetes have type 2. With type 2 diabetes, the pancreas can make insulin, but the body cannot use it properly, and so glucose cannot get into the cells. This condition is called insulin resistance. The blood glucose builds up to dangerous levels in the blood and starts to produce symptoms of diabetes.

In the past, most people with type 2 diabetes were adults. It used to be called "adult onset diabetes" for this reason. However, more and more children are developing this version of diabetes, so it is now simply called "type 2." About 19–20 million Americans have type 2 diabetes.

Type 2 diabetes can take many years to develop. People in this developing stage are called prediabetic—their blood glucose levels are higher than normal but not yet in the diabetic range. They are becoming insulin resistant and will develop diabetes unless they take steps to stop the process.

Can Sugar Cause Diabetes?

Many people have the mistaken idea that eating too much sugar causes diabetes. Since diabetes used to be called Sugar Disease and is so closely linked with the blood sugar called glucose, it is easy to see the reason for this mistake. But evidence shows that simply eating lots of sugar does not cause diabetes.

According to family practitioner John Messmer, "A much bigger problem is that people are substituting refined sugar for fresh food and consuming sugary foods rather than whole grains, fruits and vegetables. Whole grain bread is better than donuts, whole grain cereal is better than sugary kids' cereals, and fresh fruit is better than syrup laden canned fruit."

In fact, eating too much of anything—carbohydrates, fats, or proteins—can make you fat, and being overweight can cause diabetes. For overall health, eating a healthy diet with moderate amounts of a wide variety of wholesome foods is best. And do not forget the exercise.

John Messmer, "The Lowdown on Sugar: Is Sugar as Unhealthy as Everyone Claims?" www.thedietchannel.com/the-Low-down-on-sugar.htm.

The idea that someone can develop diabetes simply by eating too many sugary foods is a common misconception.

People with type 2 have a strong genetic tendency to develop diabetes. This means they often have one or more relatives who also have type 2. However, other causes also play a big role, especially being obese and having an inactive lifestyle. Too much fat interferes with the muscles being able to use insulin, and lack of exercise only makes it worse.

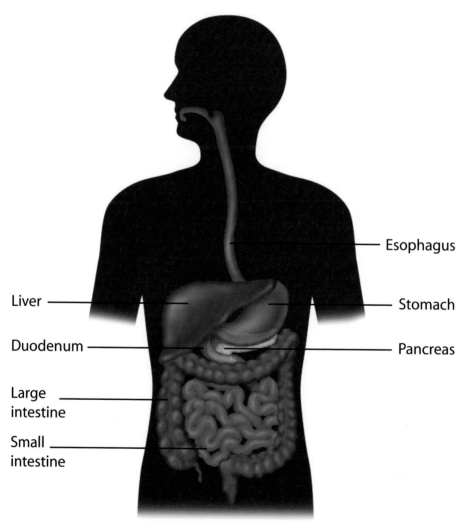

A diagram of the human digestive system includes the pancreas, which creates the hormone insulin in order to help the body process glucose.

Actor Mark Consuelos, who is married to actress Kelly Ripa, does not look like he could develop type 2 diabetes. He is slender and healthy, eats properly, and works out regularly. However, his grandfather died of complications from type 2, and his father, great aunt, aunt, and cousin all have it. In addition, he is Hispanic, an ethnic group with high numbers of type 2 diabetics. So he has pledged to maintain his healthy, active lifestyle in the hope that he will not develop the disease.

Fortunately, if he should be diagnosed with type 2 later in life, he has good role models in his family for successfully managing diabetes. His father, diagnosed in 2001, is still "able to participate in activities such as aerobics, weight training, and taking walks with his grandchildren,"[10] he says.

Many times, people with type 2 diabetes can bring their illness under control by losing weight and maintaining a healthy diet and getting more exercise. Sometimes they have to take insulin as well, but not always.

Some people are not able to control their diabetes, or they do not realize the terrible consequences of not controlling it. Becky Allen remembers her grandmother and her great aunt, who developed type 2 in middle age and did not eat a healthy diet. In fact, they so loved sugary foods, they would eat too much of them and then manipulate their insulin to make up for the rise in the blood glucose levels. This is a dangerous thing to do. Becky remembers what happened to her beloved grandmother and aunt: "As they aged and their bodies manifested the cumulative results of denial—the heart disease, excess weight, progressive loss of vision, the terribly long healing process from any casual injury or broken bone (of which there were many), poor circulation, and the attendant terror of some related amputation—they came too late to any recognition of how the choices they had made impacted their health."[11]

Type 1 Diabetes

When someone's pancreas cannot make insulin, the person has type 1 diabetes. This type of diabetes occurs mainly in children, and so it used to be called juvenile diabetes. However, as more cases have been found in adults, the term "juvenile" has been dropped from the name and replaced with "type 1." About 10 percent of Americans with diabetes have this type. That is an estimated 850,000 to 1.7 million people, with about 125,000 of those being age nineteen and under.

Type 1 diabetes is usually an autoimmune disease. This means that the immune system makes a mistake and begins attacking healthy body parts. Normally, the immune system produces antibodies that destroy bad viruses and bacteria that get into the body, like an army rushing out to stop an invading enemy. For instance, when someone gets a cut on the hand, the immune system immediately starts making antibodies that rush to the cut to prevent infection.

However, with an autoimmune illness, the immune system goes haywire. No one knows why, but it mistakenly sees healthy cells as an enemy and attacks them. When it destroys the beta cells in the pancreas, the body can no longer produce any insulin at all, creating type 1 diabetes.

Alyssa Brandenstein of Evansville, Indiana, was diagnosed with type 1 right around her thirteenth birthday. She had been an energetic, straight-A student all through school, but then mysteriously, "I was always tired, school was harder to understand, and I just wanted to go to sleep all the time. I didn't feel happy,"[12] she said.

Then she suddenly lost a lot of weight over a couple of weeks, and "there was a big change in her,"[13] says her mother, Mindy. Alyssa's doctor ordered a blood test, which discovered the diabetes, and she developed a condition called ketoacidosis, which can be life-threatening if not treated. Her family rushed her to the hospital, where she was treated for three days in January 2007. While she was there, she and her family received intense training on how to deal with this new situation.

When Alyssa first got sick, she was scared because she did not know what was wrong with her. But when she got her diagnosis of type 1, "I was happy, too, because I knew I would get better," she says. "And I had lots of people to help me."[14]

Today, with proper care, Alyssa is leading much the same life she did before her diagnosis. She and her friend even made a video about her illness, titled "Alyssa's Dream," and put it on YouTube.

Ethnic Groups and Type 2 Diabetes

Various ethnic groups in the United States have different rates of diabetes, mainly due to cultural, societal, and environmental reasons. Genetics had also been thought to play a large role, but a recent study by Australian and U.S. researchers seems to have changed that belief.

"When it comes to diabetes, we're finding that genes are no more important for ethnic minorities than for anyone else," said Stephanie Fullerton, a population geneticist and bioethicist at the University of Washington and coauthor of the study. Factors such as poor diet, housing segregation, and poverty were stronger indicators of the disease than genetic inheritance.

According to the Minority Organ Tissue Transplant Education Program:

- Native Americans have the highest rates of diabetes not only in this country but in the world. This means that the disease and its complications are major causes of death and health problems for them. Amputations, a complication of diabetes, are three to four times higher in Native Americans than in other ethnic groups.

- African Americans are 1.7 times more likely to have diabetes than whites. One-third of the 2.3 million African Americans who have diabetes do not know it, which means they are already beginning to suffer from its complications without treatment.

- Latinos/Hispanic people have twice the rate of type 2 diabetes as whites, with 1.2 million of them having the disease. About 24 percent of Mexican Americans in the United States have type 2 diabetes.

Quoted in "No Sign That Ethnic Groups' Genes Cause Diabetes," *ScienceDaily*, April 16, 2007. www.sciencedaily.com/releases/2007/04/070416132455.htm.

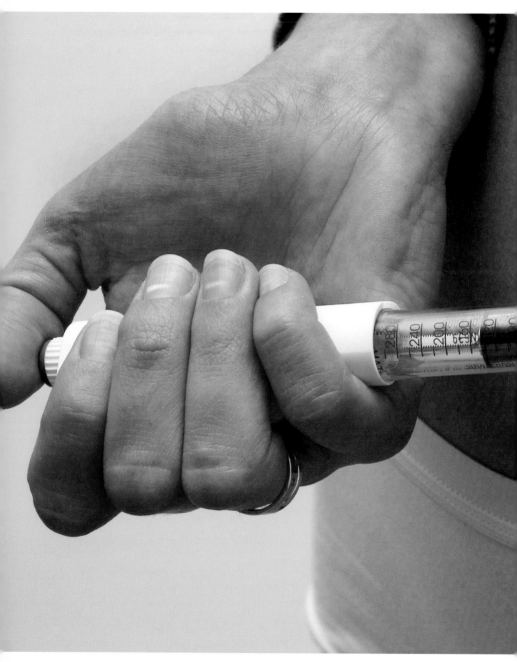

Because their bodies do not make enough natural insulin, people with type 1 diabetes manage their blood glucose levels by injecting the hormone several times a day.

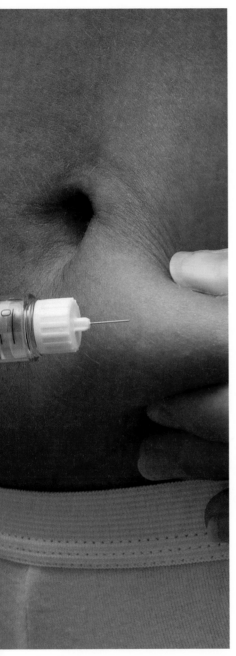

People with type 1 diabetes *must* take insulin shots several times each day to replace the natural insulin their bodies are no longer making. For that reason, type 1 is sometimes called insulin-dependent diabetes. Alyssa gives herself four insulin shots a day.

Two Other Types of Diabetes

Researchers and doctors now have a name for the kind of diabetes that combines qualities of both types 1 and 2 diabetes. Adults who are diagnosed with diabetes, but are not overweight, have very little resistance to insulin and do not immediately need insulin treatment. They are said to have Latent Autoimmune Diabetes in Adults (LADA), or type 1.5 diabetes. Sometimes people who are first thought to have type 2 are later found to have type 1.5. About 15 percent of diabetics have this type.

The other type of diabetes is called gestational diabetes. "Gestation" or "gestational" refers to the time of pregnancy. Therefore, gestational diabetes happens when a woman is pregnant, and it can happen even if she did not have diabetes before. If left untreated, it can harm the mother as well as the baby. About 4 percent of pregnant women develop this condition. This kind of diabetes disappears after the baby is born, although more

A pregnant woman prepares to check her blood glucose level. About 4 percent of women develop gestational diabetes during their pregnancies.

than half of the women who develop this type while they are pregnant will develop type 2 diabetes later in life.

These four types of diabetes all occur when something goes wrong with the pancreas and its ability to produce insulin or the body's ability to use insulin in the proper way. This serious illness is affecting more and more people in the United States and around the world. Fortunately, modern medicine has developed many new treatments and medications that can help people with diabetes live better and longer.

CHAPTER TWO

Diagnosis and Drug Treatment

When someone's pancreas stops producing insulin, which creates type 1 diabetes, the person will develop signs of the disease in weeks or months. This is what happened to Nick Jonas, one of the three New Jersey brothers who make up the popular Jonas Brothers band.

In 2005, when Nick was twelve, he noticed he was having "the usual symptoms: losing weight, the bad attitude, being thirsty, going to the bathroom all the time,"[15] he said. For several weeks, weight practically fell off of him, and "it was just insane," he explained. "I had a terrible attitude, which was totally odd for me because I'm actually a nice person."[16]

He took time out from the band's tour and saw a doctor, who sent him to the hospital. Nick was diagnosed with type 1 diabetes and put on insulin. Until this time, he had always been a healthy person.

On the other hand, type 2 diabetes creeps up slowly over decades. As someone becomes more overweight and less active, and for other reasons, the insulin produced by his or her pancreas becomes less able to help flush excess glucose out of the body. Often, a person can be prediabetic and have this faulty glucose tolerance for many years with no outward symptoms. However, even though the blood glucose level is not high

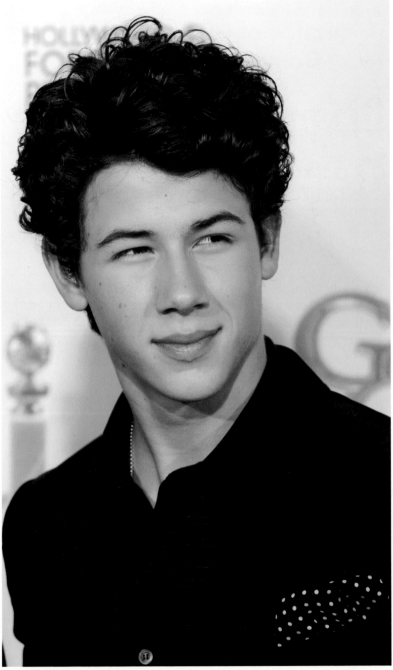

Singer Nick Jonas of the Jonas Brothers band was diagnosed with type 1 diabetes in 2005.

Rates of Risk Factors for Complications per 100 Adults with Diabetes

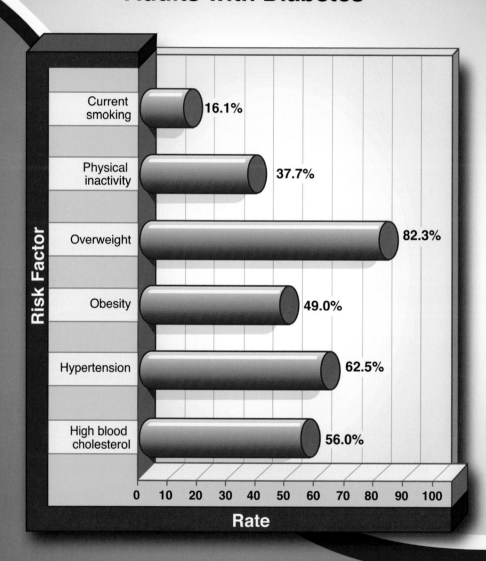

Taken from: Center for Disease Control and Prevention, http://www.cdc.gov/diabetes/statistics/.

enough to be in the diabetic range, it is higher than the healthy range and can begin causing damage to every cell in the body. When diabetes is finally diagnosed, harm has already been done to the eyes, kidneys, and other organs.

The symptoms of diabetes are now fairly well known. This is important because the sooner the illness is diagnosed, the sooner treatment can begin.

Symptoms of Type 1 Diabetes

When the human body senses that something is not working right, it will try to find a way to fix the problem. When the body cannot absorb all the glucose traveling in the bloodstream, it pulls the extra sugar, along with water, out of the blood and puts it in the urine. Then it gets eliminated in large quantities, many times day and night. This means a person with type 1 diabetes will have to urinate *a lot*.

Then, as a person with diabetes continues to urinate too much, the body loses water and begins to dehydrate, just like a sponge drying up. This is a dangerous condition, since water makes up a large percentage of the human body. The brain is 70 percent water, the lungs are 90 percent water, and so is nearly 83 percent of our blood. As too much water leaves the body, the person becomes very thirsty and keeps drinking more liquid.

Since the body is eliminating a lot of glucose in the urine, its usual source of energy from food is very low. But it knows that plenty of energy is stored in the muscles and fat, so it starts breaking them down as it searches for energy. This extreme breakdown of muscle and fat soon can make a person with diabetes dangerously thin and very sick. Like Jonas, people with uncontrolled diabetes lose weight very fast without trying. Nick lost 15 pounds (7kg) in three weeks. However, since the glucose does not have insulin to help it enter the cells, the body's cells will actually be starving for energy. This makes a person feel very hungry much of the time, despite frequently eating large amounts of food.

Due to all these conditions, a person with undiagnosed or uncontrolled type 1 diabetes will often feel extremely weak.

The muscles and the brain cannot get the energy they would normally get from glucose.

Some people with type 1 diabetes may experience what is called diabetic ketoacidosis—a long name for a dangerous condition that has two causes. First, too much of the fat in their bodies breaks down in order to supply the energy they would normally get from blood glucose. This forms ketone bodies that accumulate in the blood, which can cause nausea, abdominal pain, and vomiting. Then, as their glucose levels rise to very high levels, their blood becomes very thick (remember that water is being taken out of the blood and put into the urine), and it cannot circulate very well through the body. The combination of all these things causes extreme drowsiness and loss of consciousness. If this situation is not quickly remedied, the person could die.

Symptoms of Type 2 Diabetes

Some people with type 2 diabetes have few or no symptoms for a long time, but they will eventually develop various symptoms. Just as with type 1 diabetes, people with type 2 urinate frequently and have great thirst. They also feel weak and tired. In addition, diabetes harms the white blood cells, which help the body heal and prevent infections. Therefore, having type 2 diabetes means that infections of the skin, gums, and urinary tract heal very slowly. Blurry vision can also occur because as levels of blood sugar rise and fall, the eyes swell and shrink. Since they cannot easily adjust to these changes, the vision blurs as a result. Yeast infections thrive in environments with lots of glucose, such as in a body with type 2 diabetes, so genital itching that lasts for a long time is a common symptom of type 2.

Sixty percent of people with diabetes have some problem with their nervous system. Type 2 diabetes harms the nervous system by causing a condition called neuropathy. When neuropathy damages the nerves in the feet or legs, they can become numb, tingly, or very sensitive to touch. This can lead to serious infections and even amputation of the limbs. Neuropathy takes a long time to develop, often ten years or more, and no symptoms may appear for a long time, even though damage to the

Excessive thirst is one of the symptoms of diabetes, because the disease causes the body to become dehydrated as it pulls extra sugar and water from the bloodstream and eliminates them through urination.

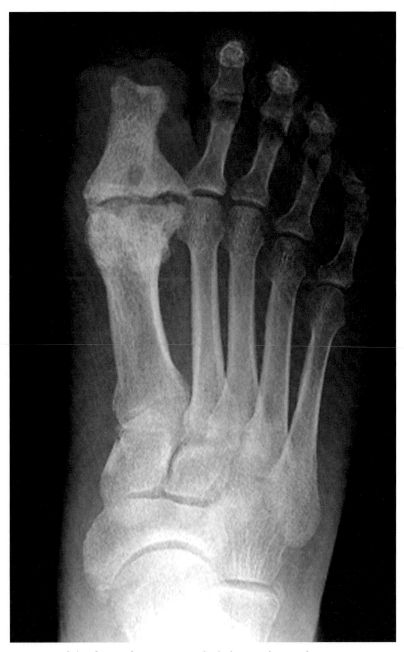

An X-ray of the foot of a person with diabetes shows the amputation of the top portion of the big toe and joint degeneration due to nerve damage. This can result when type 2 diabetes is left undiagnosed or unmanaged.

body is already occurring. It can sometimes be reduced or even healed when blood sugar is brought down to normal levels.

A serious complication of type 2 diabetes is cardiovascular disease, or heart attacks and strokes. They strike people with diabetes twice as much as people without diabetes. Diabetes can alter some of the substances in the blood, which can cause the blood vessels to narrow or clog up. This is called hardening of the arteries, which leads to stroke or heart attack.

Symptoms of Other Forms of Diabetes

People with type 1.5 diabetes are usually adult but do not have all the symptoms of type 2, so some doctors and researchers are beginning to call this late onset type 1 diabetes. These people may be thin and active, yet it is difficult for their bodies to control glucose levels. In its early stages, type 1.5 does not require

Metabolic Syndrome

About 47 million adults in the United States have a group of risk factors, called metabolic syndrome, that can increase the chances of developing diabetes as well as heart disease and stroke. The five conditions, which must occur together to be considered metabolic syndrome, are:

- Obesity in the abdomen, resulting in a body being "apple-shaped."

- A higher than normal level of the fat in the blood called triglycerides.

- A lower than normal level of "good" cholesterol, called HDL (high density lipoprotein).

- High blood pressure, or taking medicine to control high blood pressure.

- Higher than normal fasting blood glucose, or being on medicine to treat it.

insulin, but it often quickly leads to type 2 and requires insulin. Often, gestational diabetes has no symptoms, or they are mild and not threatening. If a pregnant woman does have symptoms, they may include blurry vision, increased thirst and urination, fatigue, nausea and vomiting, and weight loss even with increased appetite. Typically, blood glucose levels return to normal after the baby is born.

This condition must be treated not only for the mother's sake, but also to protect the baby from developing harmful conditions. Before birth, the baby's heart may experience extra stress. The baby may be born very large and with extra fat, which makes delivery more dangerous for both the baby and the mother. The baby might also have a condition called spina bifida, in which the spine is deformed. Right after birth, the baby may have extremely low blood glucose, and breathing problems may be another complication.

Diagnosing Diabetes

Doctors use several tests to check for diabetes and prediabetes in their patients. All of them require that blood be drawn and tested in a medical lab. The first one is called the fasting plasma glucose (FPG) test. This test measures a person's blood glucose after eight hours of not eating or drinking anything. The FPG is most reliable when it is done in the morning, and it is also the most convenient of the three tests for diabetes or prediabetes. If the fasting glucose level is 99 mg/dL (milligrams per deciliter) or below, the person does not have diabetes. If the level is 100–125 mg/dL, the person has a kind of prediabetes called impaired fasting glucose. This person does not have type 2 diabetes yet but is likely to develop it later.

If the fasting glucose level is 126 mg/dL or higher, the doctor will perform the test again to confirm the results. If the same results appear the second day, the person has diabetes.

The oral glucose tolerance test (OGTT) is another measure of blood glucose after fasting for eight hours as well as two more hours after the person drinks a liquid containing glucose.

After eight hours of fasting, blood is drawn and its glucose level is measured to provide a baseline number. Then the person drinks a special beverage of glucose dissolved in water. Two hours later blood is drawn again, and the glucose level is checked once more.

A blood glucose level of 140–199 mg/dL two hours after the drink means the person has a form of prediabetes called impaired glucose tolerance and is likely to develop diabetes in the future. If the level is 200 mg/dL or higher, the test will be performed again the next day. If the results are again 200 mg/dL or higher, the person has diabetes.

A glucometer measures a glucose level of 174 mg/dL (milligrams per deciliter) in a sample of blood, indicating impaired glucose tolerance.

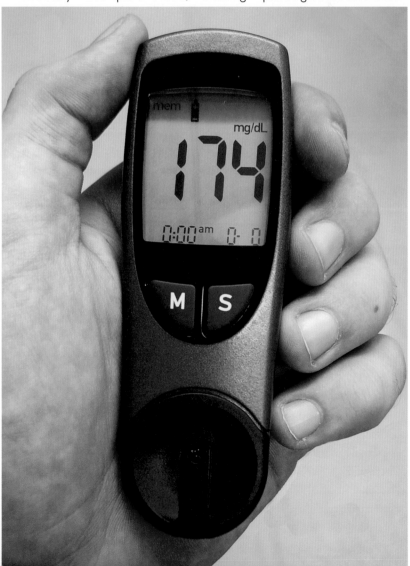

The OGTT is also used to diagnose gestational diabetes, except that blood glucose levels are checked four times during the test. If levels are higher than normal in at least two of the four checks, the woman has gestational diabetes.

The third test is the random plasma glucose test. The blood glucose level is checked regardless of when the person last ate. This test is only for diagnosing diabetes. A person can have diabetes if the blood glucose level is 200 mg/dL or higher and also has symptoms including increased urination and thirst, weight loss for no known reason, and also is experiencing increased hunger, sores that will not heal, blurred vision, and fatigue. If this is the case, the person should undergo either the FPG or the OGTT to verify the diagnosis.

Monitoring Blood Sugar

Successfully treating diabetes requires different strategies for the various types, and people with the illness must do what is best for them within those strategies. But two things are crucial: monitoring blood glucose levels and, in many cases, using insulin and perhaps other drugs.

Even diabetics who are able to carefully control their glucose can experience a wide range in levels, depending on many variables such as what they have eaten, their activity and stress level, illness, and the amount of sleep they get. Therefore, all people with diabetes *must* check their blood sugar several times a day and monitor its levels closely. First of all, people who can keep their blood glucose levels at ideal levels will feel

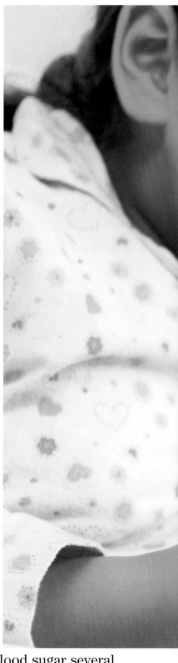

A young girl measures her blood glucose level with the assistance of a nurse in order to properly manage her medicine, food intake, and activity levels.

better and have more energy, and they can also prevent or hold off diabetic complications longer. According to the National Institutes of Health, ideal blood glucose levels are 70 to 130 mg/dL before meals and less than 180 mg/dL one to two hours after the start of a meal.

A check of blood sugar levels must be done several times a day. The number of times is determined by the type of diabetes, the kind of treatment used, and how stable the person's glucose levels usually are.

People with type 1 or 2 who are taking insulin need to test before each meal and at bedtime. Why? These checks will give them the information they need to adjust their insulin dose. People with diabetes cannot know how well they are controlling their blood glucose, no matter how well they feel, unless they do these frequent checks. For most people with type 2 diabetes, testing just twice daily—before breakfast and dinner—gives enough information if blood glucose levels are fairly stable.

Checking blood glucose can also be helpful at other times— for instance, after trying a food not normally on one's diet—to see how it affects glucose levels. Before exercise is another good time. The test will reveal whether eating before exercising is a good idea or if exercise can be used to bring down the level. Finally, if a diabetic person has been experiencing unstable glucose levels and is about to drive, a test beforehand will reveal if hypoglycemia might be a problem. Hypoglycemia can cause the brain to not function as well as it normally does, which can be dangerous while driving.

Checking one's blood sugar levels requires a tiny sample of blood, usually from a fingertip. It is taken with a lancet, which is similar to a small needle and now often built into blood glucose meters. The lancet penetrates the skin just enough to get a drop of blood. Using the side of a finger is recommended, since the sides are less sensitive than the tips, as well as changing fingers often, so any one finger does not get sore or too sensitive.

Then the sample is placed on a test strip, also stored in the meter, which is coated with special chemicals that react with the glucose. The test strip is placed in the glucose meter for the reading, and the number will show on a small screen.

A1c Test

Another important test for blood glucose is performed by a doctor to show a person's blood sugar levels over the past two or three months. It is called the hemoglobin A1c test.

Hemoglobin, a red protein that carries oxygen in the bloodstream, attaches to glucose to form hemoglobin A1c. By testing for this, a diabetic person and the physician can look back in time and see if blood glucose levels were well controlled or not. If they are well controlled, the person is more likely to avoid complications such as blindness or neuropathy. Also, it will show if treatment is working by showing improvement in glucose levels. If the treatment is not working, the doctor and the person will know it needs to be adjusted.

Taking Insulin

The major treatment for type 1 diabetics is replacing the insulin that their bodies can no longer make. Several times daily, they receive insulin through injections they give themselves or through a small computerized pump worn at the waist that automatically injects insulin under the skin at the right times. These insulin pumps are already common. In the United States they are worn outside the body on a belt or waistband; in Europe, one version that can be implanted inside the body has been approved for use. In the waistband model, insulin is delivered inside the body through a small tube called a catheter. The implanted version goes under the skin and is refilled with insulin every few months. Some people with type 2 take insulin, too, but often they can regulate their blood sugar by eating healthy foods, exercising, losing weight, and not smoking.

When insulin for use by diabetics was first created, it was made from pig and cow pancreases, so it was not very pure and the quality was often bad. Fortunately, modern medicine can now produce synthetic insulin of the highest quality and purity from genetically engineered bacteria. It is identical to the insulin created by the human pancreas.

This manufactured insulin is also made in four types that act differently in the body in three ways. First is onset, or how long

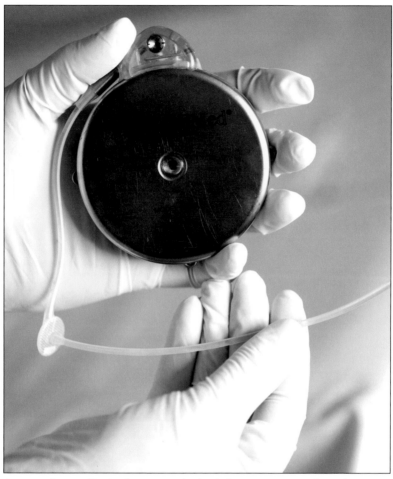

Among the medical advances to help diabetics manage their disease is an insulin pump that is implanted under the skin, providing an automatic dose of insulin as needed and eliminating the need for daily injections.

after injection the insulin begins to work. Second is peak, or how long after injection the insulin reaches maximum effectiveness. Third is duration, or how long the insulin remains effective.

The four basic types of insulin each have their own onset, peak, and duration. It is common for people with diabetes to use these four types of insulin in various combinations to better manage their illness. The rapid-acting type begins working

Are Insulin Pumps Risky for Teens?

Scientists from the Food and Drug Administration (FDA) have found that insulin pumps may pose risks for adolescents. Their review discovered thirteen deaths and more than fifteen hundred injuries related to the pumps over a decade. Sometimes the pump did not work correctly, but teens also took risks with their pumps or were careless, dropping their pumps or not taking proper care of them. Two teens may have tried to commit suicide by giving themselves too much insulin through their pumps.

Teens like the pumps, which are worn on the body and send insulin into the body through a tube inserted under the skin, because they eliminate the need to inject insulin manually several times a day. However, teens using the pumps must still frequently

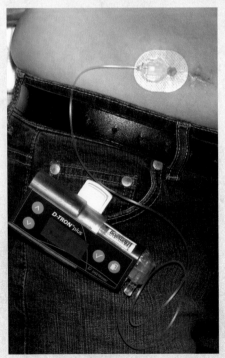

monitor their blood sugar and adjust their insulin intake through the pump. Doctors are advised to carefully screen their diabetic teen patients to make sure they are able to use and care for their insulin pumps correctly.

Because diabetic teens can be prone to misusing or being careless with insulin pumps, doctors are careful to screen their young patients to ensure they can manage a pump responsibly before prescribing it for use.

in 15 minutes, peaks in 30–90 minutes, and has a duration of 3–4 hours. The short-acting type begins working in 30–60 minutes, peaks in 2–3 hours, and has a duration of 3–6 hours. The intermediate-acting type begins working in 90 minutes to 6 hours, peaks in 4–14 hours, and has a duration of up to 24 hours. Last, the long-acting type begins to work in 6–14 hours and has a duration of 24–26 hours.

Other Medications

Many people with diabetes take oral medications along with insulin or alone to better manage their condition. These medications come in various categories, based on type, and each works differently. They can have side effects, including upset stomach, low blood glucose, weight gain, liver failure, headache, and fluid retention. They must be taken as prescribed and under a doctor's care. Studies have shown that diabetes and its complications might be prevented by these oral medications. This is especially true when the person taking them also eats a healthy diet and gets adequate regular exercise.

Avoiding Complications

Thinking about the possible complications of diabetes can be frightening. No one wants to believe they could go blind or have a foot or leg amputated or suffer from kidney failure. Yet, understanding the complications of diabetes soon after diagnosis is the best way to begin preventing them. Maintaining a healthy, proper diet, exercising regularly, and monitoring blood glucose as often as needed are the best first steps.

Additional steps must be taken to delay or prevent the onset of diabetic complications. No one, including people with diabetes, should smoke. Smoking damages the heart and narrows the blood vessels, which are already under stress from the diabetes. Blood pressure must be kept low. Hypertension, or high blood pressure, puts a strain on the body and can cause eye disease to progress faster. Losing weight and exercising, limiting salt for some people, and medications can all lower blood pressure.

People with diabetes should have annual physicals and regular eye exams to spot early signs of complications. They should also get good dental care. Gum infections are common in people with diabetes. Flossing, brushing, and regular dental exams can prevent them. Feet can be a victim of diabetes because cuts and blisters can easily become infected and be slow to heal. Feet should be washed daily in lukewarm water, dried gently, and moistened with lotion. They should be checked daily for blisters, cuts, swelling, and redness.

Drinking alcohol in moderation and always with a meal, for those who drink it (and who are old enough), will help prevent highs and lows in blood sugar. Keeping stress levels as low as possible will help the body to keep insulin working properly.

For people with diabetes, the first step in taking care of themselves is receiving a diagnosis with one of the reliable tests available today. Once the diagnosis has been confirmed, the use of insulin and perhaps oral medications, closely supervised by a doctor, will help them keep their illness under control.

CHAPTER THREE

Managing Diabetes

Managing diabetes requires consistent, responsible self-care. Many people with diabetes have lived a long time by taking proper care of themselves—eating right, monitoring their blood glucose faithfully, and exercising consistently. One is Gladys Dull, now in her nineties, who has outlived her four nondiabetic siblings, according to diabetes expert Sheri Colberg. She became friends with Gladys during interviews for her book *50 Secrets for the Longest Living People with Diabetes*. Robert and Gerald Cleveland, brothers who are both around age ninety, have also lived longer than their younger brother, says Colberg, and one of them still often goes for 20-mile bike rides (32km). Like Gladys and the Clevelands, many of the other people Colberg interviewed for the book showed her that "attention to health and lifestyle has a positive effect."[17] In other words, living well with diabetes is all about self-management.

Colberg knows how true that is. She has had type 1 diabetes since she was four. It has complicated her life, but she also has a fulfilling, productive life. At age forty-four she is an author, lecturer, professor, exercise physiologist, and expert on exercise and diabetes. She is also a mother, wife, and enthusiastic exerciser. Even with diabetes, "the world is still open to you," she says. "But it is work, and you have to be aware and plan ahead, like taking your blood glucose meter and medications along wherever you go."[18]

Diabetes management has several key components: weight, nutrition, exercise, and adequate sleep. But the first important task is to learn about Diabetes Self-Management Education and Support.

Diabetes Self-Management Education and Support

Once Colberg was old enough to understand her diabetes, she was afraid she would die at a young age from its complications—that is what the medical literature of the 1970s and 1980s told her. Today, those fears are gone. New research has brightened the picture and vastly improved the lives of people with diabetes, yet this diagnosis is still frightening and confusing. Diabetes is a serious, chronic disease that can lead to terrible complications. Therefore, it is important that newly diagnosed people be educated about diabetes self-management. Ideally, this program is presented by their health care teams, and many resources are also available elsewhere from books, the Internet, and support groups.

The main focus of Diabetes Self-Management Education (DSME) is giving people the facts and training needed to maintain physical health. This lifesaving program teaches patients how to check their blood sugar, how to eat and when, how to inject themselves with insulin, how to recognize and treat low and high blood sugar, and where to buy diabetes medications and supplies and how to store them. Often, the family is involved, as was the case with Alyssa Brandenstein and Nick Jonas. This way, they can support their loved one in the crucial task of managing diabetes.

However, once the initial education is done, people with diabetes may find it difficult to continue doing what must be done for their lifetimes. They can get discouraged or tired of having to check their blood sugar or watch what they eat. As Colberg found out in her own life, often "the problem is not so much the physical issues as the emotional ones. Diabetes crosses the physical body, the psyche, everything."[19]

A health care worker counsels elderly diabetics on the details of managing the disease, including monitoring blood sugar levels, using insulin and other medical supplies, and watching their diet and exercise.

In light of this, an additional program can give ongoing support to people with diabetes. It is called Diabetes Self-Management Support (DSMS). In this approach, people with diabetes work with their health care team and often with a support group of other people with diabetes to become more self-reliant in managing their illness. Rather than feeling overwhelmed by their disease, DSMS can help them feel more empowered to handle it safely and well. They learn together how to solve problems they face with their illness and receive support from others who understand. In addition, they are more likely to eat right more often, create better exercise habits, and set goals for themselves, such as exercising and eating correctly, that keep them feeling better physically and emotionally. Family workshops or camps for kids with diabetes are helpful for this kind of support.

Weight Watching and Nutrition

Fat helps cause diabetes because too much of it interferes with the way insulin operates in the body. This is especially true for "apple-shaped" people who carry most of their weight around the abdomen, but people who are "pear-shaped," with their weight around their hips, are also at risk. However, once diabetes develops, even a modest weight loss can help to control it.

Skipping Insulin for Weight Loss Can Be Deadly

A deadly trend has developed among some girls and young women with type 1 diabetes: They skip insulin to lose weight. However, the results of this foolhardy practice can be life-threatening.

The first effects of insulin skipping can be nausea, depression, and exhaustion that become worse over time. One young diabetic patient went blind and another suffered kidney failure as a result of avoiding their insulin. Other complications, including coma and death, can result.

This behavior is common among diabetic teen girls and young women with an eating disorder called bulimia. Usually, people with bulimia repeatedly eat huge amounts of food and then force themselves to vomit. However, diabetic girls who do not take enough insulin can eat anything they want and still lose pounds without throwing up. Doctors have begun calling them "diabulimics" and say that this behavior affects approximately one-third of all diabetic young women.

Sadly, many girls and women who forgo their insulin in order to stay thin will have shorter life spans because of the terrible stress this puts on the body.

People with diabetes need a plan that lets them safely choose the right amounts and kinds of food. By using sound guidelines to plan their meals and snacks, based on their own lives and activities, they will better control their blood glucose. In addition to helping them lose pounds or maintain a healthy weight, an eating plan keeps their food balanced with insulin and other medications.

A healthy meal plan takes into account the person's likes and dislikes and food allergies. Creating a meal plan is best done with a dietitian's help. Dietitians are experts in nutrition and healthy eating. They define a healthy diet as one that includes a variety of foods from all the food groups, is high in vitamins and minerals, high in fiber, and low in processed foods. In addition, a healthy diet reduces the risk of illnesses such as diabetes, heart problems, cancer, and stroke. So, a diet that is healthy for people with diabetes is healthy for anyone. With proper planning and attention to portion size, people with diabetes can eat the same healthy and delicious foods their families do.

A diabetes counselor uses plastic food to teach diabetics about healthy food choices and proper portion sizes so that they can better manage their weight as well as their blood glucose levels.

Guidelines for a Healthy Diet

The 2005 Dietary Guidelines from the U.S. Department of Agriculture, sometimes called the new "food pyramid," contain the latest scientific understanding of nutrition. People with diabetes can use the food pyramid to create a well-balanced and nutritious eating plan.

These guidelines are based on science, and they recognize that all people have their own food needs according to their age and level of activity. For instance, a grown man who works in an office and does not exercise needs less food than another man who is a marathon runner. A teenage girl needs a different amount of food and nutrients than her younger brother. Women in their thirties have different nutritional needs than women in their seventies. All of these things are true whether or not someone is diabetic, but diabetes requires more attention to the details of eating.

The New Food Pyramid

The new food pyramid at www.mypyramid.gov breaks down foods into six groups: grains, vegetables, fruits, milk, meat and beans, and oils. Each group has foods that are better than others. For instance, whole grain bread is better than highly processed white bread. Oatmeal is better than sugary cereals. Whole fruit is better than juice.

In order of largest to smallest amounts that should be eaten daily, here are the food groups:

- Grains—Half the grains eaten daily should be whole grains. Eat at least three ounces of whole grain bread, cereal, crackers, rice, or pasta every day.

- Vegetables—Eat a variety of veggies in lots of colors for the most benefit, and eat more dried beans and peas.

- Fruits—Eat a variety, whether fresh, frozen, canned, or dried. Keep fruit juice to a minimum.

- Milk—Dairy products are important for calcium, which keeps bones strong, and other nutrients. Choose low-fat or fat-free milk, cheese, and yogurt. Other good sources of calcium are tofu, some dark green vegetables like broccoli, and calcium-enriched cereals and juices.

- Meat and beans—For lean protein, beans are unsurpassed. Choose lean meats and poultry. The best choice is a variety of fish, beans, peas, nuts, and seeds.

- Oils—Most fat should be from fish, nuts, and vegetable oils. Limit solid fats like butter, stick margarine, shortening, and lard. Avoid trans fats, which are fats manufactured by adding hydrogen to oils to make them solid. Look for the words "hydrogenated" or "partially hydrogenated" on the label. Trans fats are also a big contributor to heart disease.

Eating the right amounts of food is also important. Too many calories mean weight gain. Underestimating the number of calories in food is easy to do, particularly today when portion sizes have grown so large. Learning to closely estimate the correct portion size can be a great help in losing or maintaining weight as well as controlling blood sugar. For instance, the healthy adult portion for a steak is 3 ounces (0.1kg), or about the size of a deck of cards. One cup of salad greens is similar in size to a baseball. A half-cup serving of ice cream is the size of half a baseball.

One of the reasons Gladys Dull has done so well controlling her diabetes for many decades is because her mother helped her learn the correct portion sizes of the foods she ate. This is a skill that can be mastered, and one that is tremendously helpful for anyone wanting to maintain a healthy weight for a lifetime.

For people with diabetes, eating at the right times and coordinating insulin injections with food is also necessary. In general, they should eat the same amounts of food at the same times every day whenever possible. Since blood sugar is usually lowest upon waking up, eating a good breakfast after checking blood sugar levels is important.

People with type 1 diabetes should not skip meals because they always have insulin, which they have injected, in their bloodstream. Along with meals at regular times, a snack in

Native Americans Returning to Traditional Diet to Combat Diabetes

Native Americans have the highest rates of diabetes in the United States. To become healthy again, many tribes are returning to eating their traditional diets instead of the highly processed foods many of their people eat.

The Oneida Nation, near Green Bay, Wisconsin, has created an organic farm, orchards with thirty-seven varieties of apples, and a cannery. They began raising a herd of buffalo for their meat, which is leaner and healthier than beef.

The Oneida Indian Nation Health Department also began the "Three Sisters Nutrition Project" to improve the health of all Native Americans living in central New York. The Three Sisters are squash, beans, and corn—traditional foods in this region that the Native Americans there consider life-sustaining gifts. When planted together, these three crops also help improve and renew the soil they are grown in, which is another advantage of raising them.

Beans, squash, and corn are at the center of the Oneida Indian Nation Health Department's "Three Sisters Nutrition Project," which promotes the consumption of traditional native foods as part of a healthy diet.

midmorning and midafternoon is a good idea. A bedtime snack can also help regulate glucose levels through the night. Weight control might be more of an issue for people with type 2 diabetes, since most of them are overweight. Even a small weight loss of 10 percent of body weight can play a large role in reducing heart disease.

Exercise

Exercise is important for everyone. But for people with diabetes, it is one of the best ways to manage their illness, even for thin diabetics who tend to be less active. Humans have muscles for a reason—they were meant to use them in active ways. Regular exercise improves glucose tolerance (so blood sugar can be controlled better with less medication) and lowers cholesterol and blood pressure. It reduces the risk of life-threatening complications of diabetes. It reduces stress. It strengthens muscles, bones, and the heart, and it keeps joints flexible. It can also help people feel happier and more energetic because it causes the brain to produce natural "feel good" chemicals called endorphins.

However, people do not have to run marathons or ride a bike for hours to get enough exercise. Lots of little activities can add up to big benefits as well. For example, take the stairs or choose a parking space farther from the door to the mall or school. Vacuum the house, garden or mow the lawn, wash the car, walk the dog—they all count as physical activity, especially if done vigorously. All it takes is a minimum of thirty minutes daily, all at once or in two or three parts.

People who have been inactive for a long time should see a doctor first and get an OK to exercise. They should explain what kinds of exercise or activities they want to try. Some might be off-limits because of diabetes. For instance, for people with diabetes who have numbness or less sensation in their feet, swimming or biking might be better than walking or running. For a person with abnormal growth of blood vessels in the retina, called diabetic retinopathy, strenuous activity might cause bleeding in the eye or cause the retina to detach, which is a very dangerous condition. A softer kind of exercise would be better.

Both aerobic exercise and strength training are beneficial to people with diabetes (and to everyone else). Aerobic means "with oxygen," so aerobic exercises such as walking, swimming, or biking at a faster than normal pace get the heart pumping and oxygen flowing through the body to burn calories. Strength training with weights—even small ones—builds muscles, and bigger muscles burn more fat faster.

In any case, people are more likely to continue exercising if they enjoy it. They should also seek out a qualified exercise specialist for learning how to lift weights, use exercise equipment, or do other unfamiliar activities.

Also important is to check with a doctor about the best times to exercise. People who take insulin might need to adjust their doses or wait a while after injecting their insulin before exercising.

Exercising with Diabetes

In general, the best time to exercise is when glucose peaks, about sixty to ninety minutes after eating. This timing provides enough energy, allows calories to be burned, and avoids high blood sugar after eating. Also important is to learn how to determine the right insulin dosages before, during, and after exercise. Why? Too much insulin before a workout can lead to too-low blood sugar, or hypoglycemia, while not enough insulin can cause too-high blood sugar, or hyperglycemia. Stress and heat can affect the blood glucose/insulin balance, so these factors must also be taken into account.

A good idea is to have some carbohydrates available during exercise in case blood sugar needs to be raised quickly. Eating carbohydrates helps to prevent hypoglycemia. And exercising with a partner who knows what to do in case of a diabetic emergency can add a safety factor as well as make exercise more fun.

Diabetic Emergencies

Emergencies related to diabetes will happen to *all* people with the illness. People who have a hard time controlling their diabetes will have them more frequently than those whose diabetes

Diabetics who stay active with exercise and other vigorous activities on a regular basis, including everyday tasks such as mowing the lawn, increase their ability to successfully manage their disease and stay healthy.

Diabetics experiencing hypoglycemia, or low blood glucose levels, can get a quick dose of the sugar they need by drinking a glass of juice.

is under better control, but even those people will have one from time to time. These medical emergencies are impossible to predict, and they can be deadly. A diabetic emergency occurs when glucose levels are either too low (hypoglycemia) or too high (hyperglycemia). The best way to prevent or minimize these situations is to know what a diabetic emergency is, know how to handle it, and do everything possible to avoid it.

One common reason for diabetic emergencies is that even with the best glucose monitoring, the same dosage of insulin can have varying effects at different times. The effect depends on the kinds and amounts of food eaten, the amount of exercise and stress, and how healthy the person is.

People with type 1 more often have swings in blood glucose than people with type 2, and so may experience more emergency situations. Hypoglycemia is the most common emergency condition for people with type 1, who take insulin or medications that lower blood glucose. In people who do not have diabetes, the body naturally stops releasing insulin before blood glucose falls too low. But once insulin is injected, its action cannot be stopped. If hypoglycemia continues too long, the person could have seizures, lose consciousness, or die.

Treating Hypoglycemia

Having help available when needed is important. The person's family members, coworkers, or other trusted people should learn to recognize the symptoms of hypoglycemia and know how to treat it if necessary. Symptoms of hypoglycemia are dizziness, sweating, feeling shaky or faint, clamminess, rapid heartbeat, clumsiness, moodiness, and extreme hunger. However, each person should know his or her own particular symptoms since everyone reacts differently.

Some people eventually lose their ability to realize they are hypoglycemic. If they miss the early signs, fuzzy thinking may be the first symptom, which means they will not know how to help themselves. It is recommended that these people test blood glucose more frequently and test it before driving, wear a diabetes ID bracelet, and keep a prescription for glucagon nearby. Glucagon is a hormone that, when injected, causes the liver to release glucose, and it also slows insulin release. People with type 1 must know how to inject it and also should train someone, such as a family member or coworker, to inject it in case they are unable to do so.

In a case of severe hypoglycemia, the person must immediately eat or drink a small amount of a carbohydrate that the digestive system can quickly pick up from the bloodstream. Glucose tablets or gel from the pharmacy work well, as do raisins, regular soda, orange juice, honey, or jelly beans. These sugars should be kept at home, school, and work, in a purse or pocket, and in the car. About fifteen minutes after taking one, blood sugar should be checked. If it is still too low, another small dose of carbohydrate should be taken or a meal eaten.

Diabetics must frequently measure their blood glucose level to ensure that it is neither too high nor too low, as either extreme can cause a serious medical emergency.

Treating Hyperglycemia

The other diabetic emergency is hyperglycemia, or too much blood sugar. It is unpredictable, possibly deadly, and happens from time to time to all people with diabetes. This is more rare than hypoglycemia but still very dangerous. People with types 1 and 2 can suffer from it but react differently.

In type 1, diabetic ketoacidosis (DKA) occurs when people do not get enough insulin. The body believes it is starving and breaks down fat to get energy. This causes ketones to form in the blood, and if the body cannot release them through urine, they build up and poison the body. The body also becomes dehydrated because of frequent urination, which only increases the concentration of ketones. As ketones build up to dangerous levels, coma, shock, difficulty breathing, and death can result.

Symptoms usually come on slowly. The major DKA symptoms are dry mouth, terrible thirst, and frequent urination. Others include little appetite, blurry vision, vomiting or feeling sick to the stomach, fever, weakness, sleepiness, and fruity odor on the breath.

Someone who is hyperglycemic must have an injection of quick-acting insulin and drink lots of sugar-free liquids. If the condition does not improve rapidly, the person must seek emergency medical help. Sometimes, people who do not yet know they have type 2 diabetes can develop hyperglycemia. They and people already diagnosed with type 2 who experience this condition can have it for a long time without realizing it. Their glucose level can zoom to extremely high levels, which can lead to coma and death.

Hyperglycemia leads to a condition called HHS. It can happen to people who do not use insulin but take oral medicines. HHS symptoms are sleepiness or mental confusion, extreme thirst, no sweating, and warm skin. Also, the person will have high blood glucose levels. Seeking medical help is important when blood sugar levels are extremely high. The best way to avoid HHS is to check glucose levels at least once a day.

Managing diabetes is complicated and time-consuming, but it is necessary in order to avoid the terrible complications that can happen as a result of having this illness. Careful management includes blood glucose monitoring, insulin and sometimes other drugs, regular exercise, and a healthy diet. In addition, studies have shown that laughter and a positive attitude are good medicine for diabetes. Laughter has been found to lower glucose levels after eating. It also produces chemicals in the body that make people feel better in general, which helps make daily life easier and more pleasant.

CHAPTER FOUR

Living Well with Diabetes

Diabetes is an illness that can produce serious complications and potentially cause an early death. However, millions of people live with it every day, and live well.

A type 1 diabetic herself as well as a researcher of diabetes, Sheri Colberg has spoken with thousands of people who have the illness. The ones who have the most success at managing their diabetes do not let it take over their lives. It is a challenge that definitely affects their lives, but like Colberg, they live life first and are diabetic second.

Especially when she was interviewing people for her latest book, *50 Secrets of the World's Longest Living People with Diabetes*, she heard a common theme from her subjects, some of whom have lived with diabetes for more than eight decades. The people she spoke with did not let their diabetes control them. People with a chronic disease commonly suffer with depression and a sense of hopelessness, but "these people have gone so far beyond that, to the point of embracing diabetes,"[20] she says. They told Colberg, "Diabetes saved my life. I look around and see people so unhealthy, and I'm healthy."[21]

"Diabetes doesn't have to hold you back from much of anything," she explains, knowing this from her own life as well as from others' experience. "Diabetes can even make you stronger, because you have to take responsibility for yourself."[22]

When people are diagnosed with diabetes, they can feel overwhelmed and frightened. After all, diabetes is potentially deadly, and it has serious consequences when not controlled. Newly diagnosed people have a lot to learn about their disease and how to manage it. This is important to avoid the life-altering complications and also to live as well as possible with it. Some people never learn to manage their diabetes well, or for some reason they are not able to. Their diabetes seems to rule their lives, and they can become seriously depressed. But many people adjust well and work hard to keep their diabetes under control. This takes a lot of effort, patience, and a positive outlook. Here are the stories of four people who learned to live life first and be diabetics second.

Linda Koehler

Linda Koehler of Tucson, Arizona, developed type 1 at age eleven. She is now fifty-five. Unlike many people who keep their diabetes private, she has not been afraid to let people know about hers. She has worked as a first-grade teacher for many years, and she always makes sure her students know she has diabetes.

"If I have low blood sugar and do something like forget their names for a little while, they understand why,"[23] she explains. And should her diabetes make it necessary for her to have help from another adult, her students know to call someone.

After her diagnosis Koehler remained active and fit, riding her bike and playing lots of tennis. But she did curtail some activities such as going to restaurants or to friends' birthday parties because she could not have a piece of cake. She was afraid of her diabetes getting in the way of what she wanted to do, although she later learned it did not have to. She says she was fortunate because "my mother was always harping after me to eat the right things. She was always diligent about educating me. She guided me to know what to do and what not to do."[24] However, she could not fully accept that she had diabetes when she was young because she did not want to be different from other kids. Sometimes, she just did not want to give herself insulin shots or eat right all the time. Because of this, Koehler was frequently hospitalized when her blood sugar became too high.

Children with diabetes sometimes find that the demands of managing their disease can make it difficult to fit in with their peers.

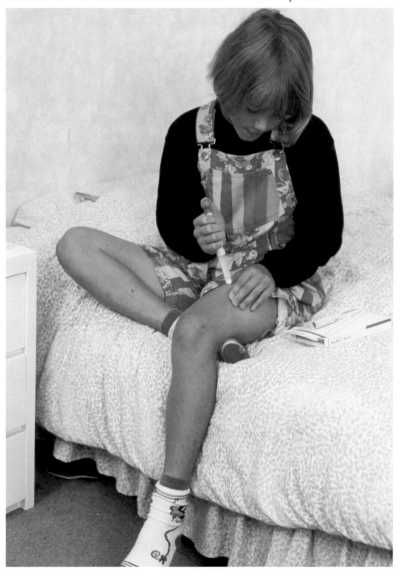

Koehler is married and has three daughters, aged 27, 20, and 11. But when she was an adolescent, she recalls, "my childhood doctor advised me in a friendly 'heart-to-heart' chat that it would not be a good idea for me to have children and pass on this horrible disease to humanity. Emotionally, this discussion hit me hard. As a result, my goal in life was to make my life as normal as I could."[25]

She is healthy, too, with none of the typical complications of diabetes, and she plans to live a very long time. She still eats well, and although she does not exercise as much as she would like, she is very active. She has not let diabetes prevent her from having a full life, always believing she can handle a new opportunity when it comes along.

When Koehler was diagnosed in the mid-1960s, and for years afterward, living with diabetes was more complicated than it is now. For instance, in those days before disposable syringes, taking insulin meant boiling glass syringes to sterilize them and fitting them with long needles for the shots. When she was pregnant with her third daughter in the late 1990s, she had

Puberty and Diabetes

As if diabetes in children is not already difficult to control, adolescence and puberty can make it even harder. All the hormonal changes under way can make blood glucose and insulin levels swing wildly, no matter how carefully the adolescent with diabetes works to stay within normal levels.

One hormone in particular is believed to be the culprit. During puberty, growth hormone stimulates bone and muscle mass to grow, and it also works to block insulin. At the same time, as blood sugar falls, another hormone called adrenaline is released into the bloodstream, which triggers the release of stored glucose. The result is that blood glucose can fluctuate up and down very quickly.

trouble regulating her blood sugar, as do many pregnant women with diabetes because of the many changes that happen to a woman's body during pregnancy. So her doctor suggested she begin using an external insulin pump, which is worn near the waist and regularly sends insulin into the body through a small tube. Using an insulin pump means not having to inject insulin. She began using a pump and found it so easy to use and so helpful in regulating her blood sugar, she soon knew she would never give it up. "It gives me a lot more convenience and makes my life a lot more normal,"[26] she says. Koehler has had many years to adjust to the fact that she has diabetes, and for a long time she has taken excellent care of herself. She still ends up in the hospital sometimes, as do many diabetics who are careful about managing their diabetes, simply because this is an unpredictable disease. Today, she is better prepared when that happens and works harder than she did in childhood to make sure it happens less often.

She has some hard-won advice for people newly diagnosed with diabetes, whether it be type 1 or 2. She says, "First, listen to the professionals," followed by, "Hands on, minds on,"[27] meaning that learning as much as possible about diabetes self-care is important. As someone who has had diabetes since childhood, she knows the importance of support from peer groups. If kids with diabetes can attend special camps or groups that teach them about diabetes and gives them an opportunity to meet other kids with the illness, that can be a huge help.

"They need to believe in themselves and do what they can to take care of themselves," she says. "It's up to them. No one else can do it for them. They have to accept that they have diabetes and persevere."[28]

Robert Mandell

Diabetes can strike at any age, and it can remain hidden for years. Fortunately, if it is type 2, eating right and exercise can help delay its onset and the use of medications to treat it, as Robert Mandell discovered.

Mandell, now eighty-five, has had type 2 diabetes for more than forty years. "I have a bad family history of it. My mother and

grandmother had it,"[29] he says. Like many people, he did not realize his blood sugar was higher than it should be until he went
for his annual physical. His doctor said test results showed Mandell's sugar was high but medication was not necessary yet.

Regular exercise can help people whose blood glucose levels run a
little higher than normal bring down their numbers and prevent a
diagnosis of diabetes.

Mandell weighed about 215 pounds then, and his doctor encouraged him to start exercising. He began taking frequent walks with a friend, and then the two of them started jogging. He lost about 30 pounds. When he moved to Florida, "My new doctor hounded me to lose more weight, and I got to 175 pounds,"[30] he says. For many years, his diabetes remained under control and he took only an oral medication for it.

Finally, when he was around seventy years old, he had to begin injecting insulin. Today, he takes both insulin and oral medication twice daily. The insulin caused him to gain some weight, and he still exercises occasionally by walking and riding a stationary bike, but "not as much as I should," he admits. While he eats pasta occasionally, he eats lots of salads because "I know what I have to do."[31] Mandell had heart surgery a few years ago and has arthritis in his hands. "Outside of that, I'm in reasonably good health for my age,"[32] he says. His biggest challenge is having to take about twelve pills every morning and night, some for diabetes and some for other conditions.

His best advice for someone newly diagnosed with type 2 diabetes is "diet and exercise. That's it," he says. "Get into an exercise program and keep your weight down. Most people who have type 2 are on the obese side. If they exercise, usually they can maintain [their health] for many years without insulin."[33]

Nicole Johnson Baker

Today, diabetes does not have to stop people from doing much of anything. With proper planning and care, combined with the exciting new medical technology available, a person with diabetes can follow his or her dreams, even all the way to a crown, as Nicole Johnson Baker did.

When Baker was diagnosed with type 1 diabetes at age nineteen in 1993, she had no idea she would later be crowned Miss America in 1999. In fact, her doctors warned her against competing in the pageant because they said the stress would be harmful.

She entered anyway. During the entire pageant, she wore her insulin pump, as she always does, and talked with many people about the illness. Now in her mid-thirties, Baker is a national diabetes consultant for the company that makes her

Nichole Johnson Baker, a type 1 diabetic, leads the pageant parade in Atlantic City, New Jersey, after being crowned Miss America in September 1999.

Hypoglycemic-Alert Dogs

Assistance dogs for people who are blind, deaf, or have other physical challenges have become a familiar addition to the range of tools that help them live safely. Now, some dogs are being trained to help people with diabetes avoid the danger of low blood sugar. Especially for very young children or people afraid of becoming hypoglycemic without realizing it, these amazing dogs are proving their worth.

Trainers of these dogs say they are right 90 percent of the time in sensing a dangerous fall in blood glucose even before the person with diabetes is aware of it. When they sense this, they "alert"—jump, run around, pace, or put their head in their owner's lap—to remind their owner to eat some appropriate food to bring glucose levels up to normal. The dog then gets a treat.

While no one yet knows how dogs do this, it is believed they are able to pick up scents created by the chemical change in their owners' bodies.

These hypoglycemic-alert dogs cost at least twenty thousand dollars, and the training of dog and client takes about two years.

Luka, a one-year-old German shepherd, sensed something was wrong when his owner, Doug Ryerson, had a diabetic emergency in 2005. The dog barked and growled in distress until help arrived, likely saving Ryerson's life.

insulin pump. She is a cohost of *dLife*, a weekly program on CNBC aimed at people with diabetes. She has written many articles about living with diabetes, her autobiography, and several cookbooks. She is also a familiar face in Washington, D.C., where she promotes legislation regarding diabetes.

She lives in Pittsburgh, Pennsylvania, with her husband, and she is pursuing a second master's degree, in public health (her first is in journalism). When she was diagnosed with diabetes, her doctors told her she should never have children because of the danger diabetes would pose to her and to the baby. Today, her daughter Ava is a healthy five-year-old.

Diabetes has certainly affected Baker's life, but it has also given her the opportunity to be a role model for empowering people with diabetes. She says, "One's greatest challenge can be one's greatest blessing, physically and psychologically."[34] In that light, she has always not only accepted her diabetes but also found it to be a blessing. By dealing with it honestly and openly, she has created a good career that revolves around it. She has also used the strength and wisdom it has brought her in her family and professional life.

In addition to her insulin pump, she sometimes wears a glucose sensor attached to her abdomen, which gives her constant blood sugar readings without the finger sticks. She has a cell phone that automatically transfers the glucose readings to her health care team. All this technology helps her feel more in control and does an excellent job of keeping her right on track.

Diabetes is life-changing. While it can often be successfully controlled, it requires constant vigilance. People who have it can never ignore that fact—because they could die if they do. Yet acceptance and a positive attitude, as Baker has shown, can go a long way in creating a happy, successful life even with diabetes.

In 2006 Baker said, "What you think will steal life away has given me life. It has taught me more than ever about determination and discipline and other things I've never been exposed to."[35]

Jay Cutler

In the past, people with serious, chronic illnesses were expected —even ordered—to remain inactive out of fear that too much activity would be harmful. They would often also hide their disease as if it were something shameful, or hide themselves from the public eye because they believed acknowledging their illness would damage their reputation. Fortunately, as Jay Cutler and other athletes are demonstrating, such beliefs are outdated.

To watch Cutler on the football field, it is impossible to know that the young, 6-foot, 3-inch (2m) quarterback for the Denver Broncos has type 1 diabetes. His throwing arm is strong, he is energetic and powerful. He is still fast on his feet. And he is working hard to remain that way. Jay was diagnosed in April 2008, after mysteriously losing thirty pounds the previous fall, along with having severe thirst, fatigue, frequent urination, and unstoppable hunger.

"I was just crushing food," he recalls. "I was eating six meals a day—I'd eat a meal and like 30 minutes later I'd be ready to eat again. Yet I kept losing weight, and they were telling me it was the stress. I was like, 'I'm not that stressed.' I mean, my jeans were falling off my body and I was all pale."[36]

Bronco coach Mike Shanahan praises Jay for taking control of his illness. "Jay has met this thing head on," Shanahan said. "I'm really not surprised. I mean, he was diagnosed with a very serious disease, and he has just gone after it and is treating it. He's done a great job of dealing with it. Jay has great discipline. To be a successful quarterback in the National Football League, you have to have discipline, and Jay has plenty of it. It is really helping him deal with it."[37]

Now the quarterback, who comes from Santa Claus, Indiana, faithfully checks his blood glucose levels and injects himself with insulin several times daily. He eats meals carefully prepared by the team's nutritional staff. His weight is back up in the 220 range, a good weight for him. He says he feels fine and does not experience many highs or lows in his blood sugar. He and the team believe he will be a better player than ever.

NFL quarterback Jay Cutler has maintained his skills on the football field despite being diagnosed with type 1 diabetes in April 2008.

Today, millions of people have diabetes. They come from all ethnic and social groups. They can be rich or poor, college graduates or uneducated, old or young. But as this very tiny sample of four people shows, having diabetes does not mean that normal life comes to an end. People with diabetes can still have good, productive lives. That does not mean it will be easy, because managing and coping with diabetes is hard work. It requires patience and determination. But oftentimes, coping with a serious illness can make people stronger and more willing to face other challenges. That is certainly true for Linda Koehler, Robert Mandell, Nicole Johnson Baker, and Jay Cutler, just as it is true for many other people with diabetes.

CHAPTER FIVE

The Future of Diabetes

Perhaps because so many more people are developing diabetes today than in the past, the search for ways to better control it, even to cure it, is being pushed even harder. In recent years diabetes care has improved tremendously because of ongoing research, new medicines, and increased knowledge about how to manage it. In addition, many people with diabetes now receive not only better medical care but counseling and emotional support not available in the past.

What does the future hold for people with diabetes? Someday, they may be able to give up injecting themselves with insulin and instead breathe it in through an inhaler, take it in a pill, or absorb it through their skin from an insulin patch. Pricking a finger to get a blood sample for a glucose reading may one day be a thing of the past, as new devices are being developed for this process. One new product now under consideration but far from actual development is called the Charmr. This small electronic device would look like a tiny iPod. It could be worn on a neck chain or around the wrist like a watch, and it would replace both the bulky insulin pump and the glucose testing meter.

Many researchers are investigating several possible new treatments for diabetes. The list includes stem cell research,

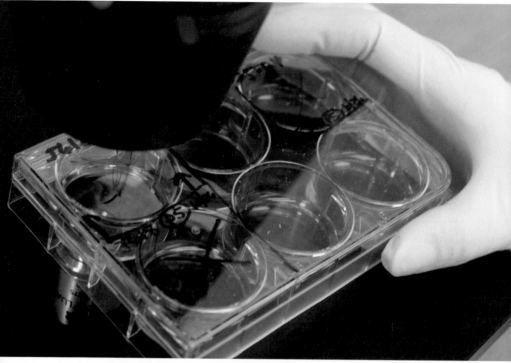

A scientist studies colonies of stem cells as part of ongoing research into the genes involved in insulin production, which may be the key to the development of advanced treatments and cures for diabetes.

tissue reengineering, islet transplantation, gene research, and development of an artificial pancreas.

Stem Cell Research

Embryonic stem cells are immature cells in animal embryos that later develop into other cells that make up all the various organs and tissues of the body, such as the heart, eyes, lungs, bones, and pancreas. Early in their development they are like blank slates, but then a process happens in the embryo to make them begin changing into those different kinds of cells. No one understands this entire process yet or how to reproduce it in the laboratory. Adults also have stem cells, but they work differently from embryonic stem cells, and they are not used for the same kind of research.

An enormous amount of research has already been done with the pancreas. Scientists have identified the "master" genes in this organ, and some of these master genes tell embryonic stem cells to become beta cells, which create insulin. Once scientists discover how to re-create this very complex process in the lab, they can then build a process to safely and reliably manufacture enough beta cells. Someday these manufactured cells could possibly be used to cure type 1 diabetes. People with type 2 might also be able to use them for better control of their illness.

Tissue Engineering

Tissue engineering is an amazing process that scientists recently developed to help replace damaged parts of the body. Someday they hope to be able to grow various organs, even hearts and lungs, in the lab for people who need transplants. However, tissue engineering is still very new, and skin is about the only body part that so far can be successfully engineered in a lab for use in humans.

Engineered skin is made by taking skin cells from a person who, for instance, has suffered severe burns and cannot re-grow enough of his or her own skin naturally to cover the burned portions. Those skin cells are used to grow pieces of new skin in a special lab. The new skin can then be grafted over the burned areas and help them heal.

It is common for people with diabetes to have cuts or wounds on their feet that do not heal, even after many months of treatment, because their illness damages the skin of the feet and legs. These wounds can become seriously infected, which can lead to amputation. It has been found that tissue-engineered skin can be used to help these wounds heal. Unlike the skin used for some burn victims, this new skin is made from tissues other than the patient's, but it works very well. The doctor carefully cleans the wound and then places the tissue-engineered skin over it. It grafts with the person's own skin, and the body restores the injured area. Treating these wounds with tissue-engineered grafts promotes faster healing more often than the usual treatment with moist dressings.

A strip of skin grown in a laboratory can be used to treat diabetics with wounds that are slow to heal.

It is also less risky and less expensive than taking live skin from a donor.

Tissue engineering also presents many opportunities for researchers looking for improved diabetes treatments or a cure. They believe that beta cells can eventually be tissue-engineered to replace the damaged or missing ones in the pancreas of a person with type 1 diabetes. These cells would be placed into the person's pancreas, where they could grow and reproduce to make adequate amounts of insulin once again.

Large-scale research in this area faces one large obstacle, though. Many millions of beta cells are needed for this research, along with a continuing supply for many years. But not enough beta cells are available to researchers (these cells come from deceased human donors). Furthermore, those donor cells that have been available have not been able to survive or maintain their ability to produce insulin in the lab for very long.

However, some of the scientists doing this research have been able to produce a "cell line" of beta cells, similar to lines of stem cells, that has shown promising results for tissue engineering. These specially created cells would be an excellent and abundant alternative to donated cells. When they were tested in diabetic mice in 2005, the new beta cells controlled the mice's blood sugar levels for just over four months and produced about 40 percent as much insulin of normal beta cells. Although these results were not permanent and need improvement, this is an excellent outcome for an early experimental treatment. However, for such a treatment to be fully tested and declared safe for humans will take years.

Islet Transplants

The islets of Langerhans are clusters of cells in the pancreas that contain beta cells, which make insulin. In a medical procedure that is still experimental, these islets are carefully removed from a deceased person's pancreas and transplanted into the pancreas of a person with severe type 1 diabetes. The results are promising but by no means perfect. "The ultimate goal of islet cell transplantation is to normalize blood glucose levels and prevent secondary complications of diabetes, such as kidney failure, heart disease, nerve damage and loss of vision,"[38] says Alan C. Farney, a transplant surgeon at the University of Maryland Medical Center.

In one study in Canada, sixty-five people with type 1 diabetes that was difficult to control received islet transplants. Five years later, only about 10 percent of those people no longer had to inject insulin. Most of the other people had to begin using insulin again after the transplanted islets gradually lost their ability to make their own. However, many of these same people had been able to reduce their use of insulin, have more stability in their levels of blood glucose, and reduce problems with hypoglycemia, or low blood sugar.

In another study of 225 patients from the United States, Canada, Europe, and Australia who received islet transplants, nearly two-thirds were able to stop injecting insulin for at least two weeks at a time during the first year after the operation. However, that number fell to only one-third two years after the surgery. Even so, many of the 225 people still required less insulin than before the transplant, had improved control of blood glucose, and greatly reduced their risk of becoming severely hypoglycemic.

However, says Farney, the islet transplant "is not a cure. It is a treatment. Patients will still have to take medicine to prevent rejection of the transplanted cells."[39] As with any transplant, rejection is the greatest risk and problem. When the body senses something inside it that it believes does not belong there, the immune system will attack it in an effort to get rid of it. With type 1 diabetes, the immune system often mistakenly destroys the person's own beta cells, and this can happen again with new islets from someone else.

That is why people who receive any kind of transplant, including islets, must take special drugs, called immunosuppressive drugs, to prevent the body from attacking and destroying the transplanted islets. These drugs must be taken for life. Unfortunately, these drugs can have terrible side effects, including mouth sores, digestive problems, anemia, and high blood pressure and cholesterol levels. Because they suppress the immune system, they make the person more likely to have infections, and

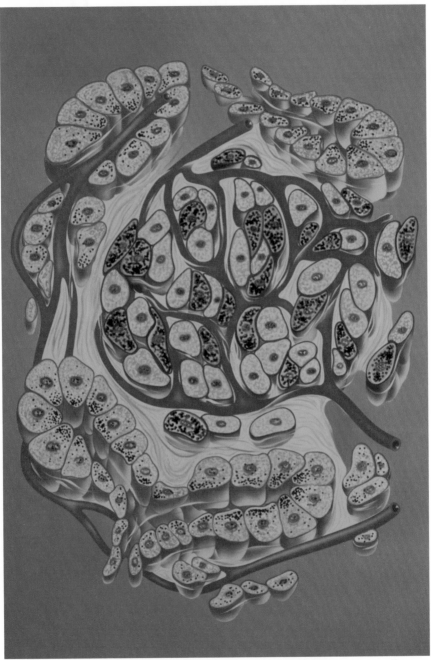

An illustration shows an islet of Langerhans, a group of pancreas cells involved in insulin production. Experimental islet transplants are showing promise as a possible treatment for diabetes.

they also increase the risk of cancer. Therefore, people who undergo islet transplantation must first understand the possible severe side effects. Researchers are continuing to look for new and better immunosuppressive drugs with fewer side effects. Their main goal is to help people who receive islet transplants to achieve immune tolerance, which would enable them to keep the new islets functioning normally without all the drugs.

As islet transplants become safer and more common, more people with type 1 diabetes will want to have the surgery. However, a great shortage of donated pancreases prevents more of these surgeries from being done. Researchers are looking for solutions to this problem, too. One possibility is to use a portion of a pancreas from a living donor, rather than from a deceased one. Not enough pancreases to meet the need are donated after death, so the hope is to find more living donors. Researchers have also experimented with injecting pig islets into other animals. Since pig organs are very similar to humans', the researchers are hoping to someday use pig islets as an abundant source for human transplants. Perhaps islet cells could also be created from stem cells or other kinds of cells, and then they could be grown in a lab.

Gene Research

Both types 1 and 2 diabetes have their roots in a person's genes, which carry DNA, or the basic building blocks of an organism, from one generation to the next. Half of a person's genes come from the mother and half from the father, and human beings have tens of thousands of them. Genes determine if people have blue or brown or green eyes, how tall they are, if they go bald, if they have the potential to develop various illnesses, and so on.

To complicate matters, just because a person has a gene linked to a certain disease, that does not mean the person will eventually develop the disease. For instance, if someone has the genes related to type 2 diabetes but maintains a healthy weight and gets enough exercise throughout his or her life, the disease may never appear.

The study of genes is still very young, so scientists still have much to learn about the human genome, or the full collection

Bones and Diabetes

A research study in 2007 showed how bones make a hormone that helps to regulate sugar and fat in the body. The scientists who did this research with mice are hopeful that this breakthrough might one day lead to a treatment or even prevention of type 2 diabetes in humans.

According to Gerard Karsenty, the lead author of the study, "What this study shows is that [the skeleton] is a lively organ that has a function to regulate the biology of the other organs in the body, such as the pancreas and insulin secretion, and fat and insulin sensitivity. . . . It is the first time the skeleton has been shown to reach out to other organs in the body."

The scientists doing this research discovered that cells that form bone, called osteoblasts, release a hormone called osteocalcin, which helps the body produce more insulin and increases insulin sensitivity. Osteocalcin also pumps up the number of beta cells in the pancreas that produce insulin while reducing fat.

It will likely be ten or fifteen years before research can show that this kind of hormone injection would be safe for humans. In the meantime, Karsenty recommends that everyone, especially people with diabetes, take care of their bones.

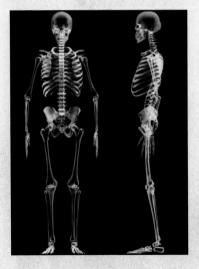

Quoted in *CBS News*, "Bones Play Key Role in Diabetes: Study," August 10, 2007. www.cbc.ca/canada/british-columbia/ story/2007/08/10/bones-insulin.html.

Bones produce the hormone osteocalcin, which helps to regulate sugar and fat in the body. Research on osteocalcin may lead to treatments for type 2 diabetes.

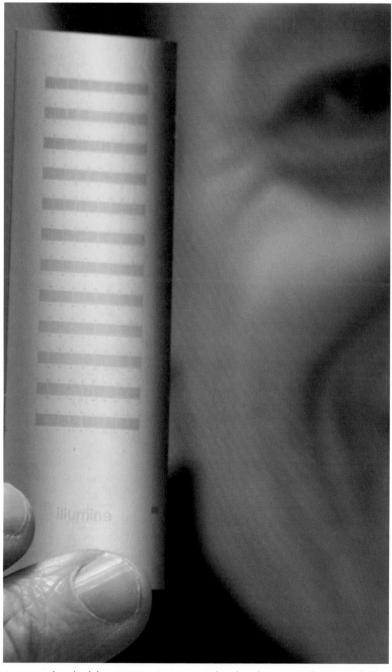

A researcher holds a DNA micro array that has been used successfully to identify genes related to type 2 diabetes.

of human genes. But one thing they do know is that diseases, including diabetes, are usually caused by multiple genes. Perhaps diseases would be easier to cure if only one gene was responsible.

Janelle Noble is a researcher at Children's Hospital Oakland Research Institute who is building a genetic database of children and families with diabetes. At a meeting of diabetes experts in 2008, she said, "If we're going to prevent diabetes we have to know who's likely to get it in the first place. But looking for variants of genes that cause complex diseases is like looking for a needle in a haystack."[40]

Research also suggests that many more varieties of diabetes than types 1, 2, 1.5, and gestational may exist. If this is the case, then the genetic basis for diabetes will be even more complicated than previously believed, and treatment could be much more personalized than it is today. Many researchers studying this are investigating questions such as, of two equally overweight people why does only one have diabetes? Or, why do some diabetics still have healthy kidneys even after decades of poor blood sugar levels, while others' kidneys are terribly damaged early on?

A gene therapy developed at Baylor College of Medicine seems to have cured diabetes in mice by coaxing their liver cells to become beta cells that produce insulin. The mice were completely cured of diabetes for at least four months. Since the liver cells came from the mice themselves, antirejection drugs were not needed. While it will be many years before this procedure can safely be used in humans, it is a very promising development.

Artificial Pancreas

An artificial pancreas would revolutionize diabetes treatment. By automatically regulating a person's blood glucose, such a device implanted under the skin would allow type 1 diabetics to keep their levels within a normal range.

Scientists are already developing an artificial pancreas and are having some success, although it is not yet ready for widespread use. This human-made pancreas has three parts: a sensor

Space Age Implantable Insulin Pumps

In 1986 Sam Zaccari, now almost seventy, had one of the first implantable insulin pumps surgically placed inside his body. In 1998 he said, "It's wonderful because without this technology that we got today I wouldn't have the control I have and maybe I might not be here."

Zaccari's insulin pump, made of titanium, was developed in part from the technology of the mechanical robot arm of the first space probe sent to Mars. The pump had a similar design to the portion of the arm the Viking spacecraft used to touch the Martian soil for experiments.

Zaccari's pump was computerized and allowed him to have more precise control of his blood glucose. He knew how important this control was, since his mother, brother, and sister had died from the complications of their diabetes. Having his pump meant he could live a more normal life and avoid their fate. Today, this Baltimore resident, nicknamed the Iron Man for his strength and longevity, still takes daily walks and has raised hundreds of thousands of dollars for diabetes research. He believes he could not have done this without his implantable insulin pump.

Quoted in Dan Rutz, "From Pacemakers to Braces, the Medical Benefits of Space Exploration," *CNN*, November 2, 1998. www.cnn.com/HEALTH/9811/02/space.medical/index.html.

to continually monitor blood glucose, an insulin pump, and a small computer that controls insulin delivery.

Insulin pumps are already in common use. The most difficult part of the device to make is the glucose sensor. None made so far offer consistently accurate results.

An artificial pancreas began undergoing tests in France in 2003. The sensor is placed in a neck vein, and it communicates with the implantable pump in the abdomen by using a wire under the skin. The pump then releases the right amount of insulin.

Results were good, with the device automatically keeping the person's blood sugar in the normal range more than half the time (although this needs to be improved) and with the risk of hypoglycemia falling to under 5 percent. The biggest problem is that the sensors stop working inside the body after about nine months and have to be replaced. This means the person using it has to undergo minor surgery again every time a replacement is needed. The sensor needs to be made out of better materials that can withstand the environment inside the body, so scientists are working on that. They believe that a safe, workable artificial pancreas will be available within the next few years.

An X-ray of the chest of a diabetic with an artificial pancreas reveals a sensor wire (left) attached to a vein in the neck that is connected to an implanted insulin pump (not seen).

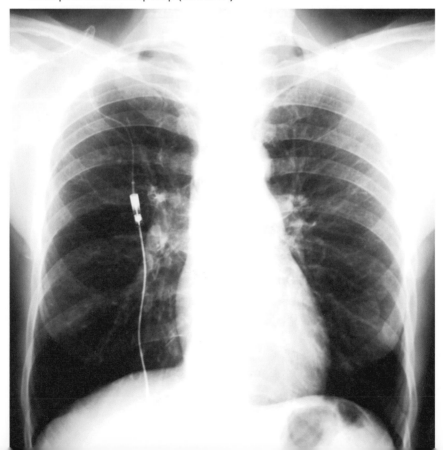

Twin Epidemics

Diabetes is a growing problem in the United States. That growth is intertwined with the increase in the number of individuals who are seriously overweight or obese. Many factors in society have brought about these twin epidemics, the largest ones being unhealthy diets and lack of physical activity. So, even though people must take responsibility for their own health, that is a difficult task without support from the larger society.

Modern medicine is developing new techniques that may someday make diabetes more manageable and easier to live with. Perhaps researchers will even find a way to reduce or stop the terrible complications of diabetes. Yet whatever miracles medicine may someday produce to help people with diabetes, there is one sure way to end this epidemic. Society must focus on helping everyone to have a healthy, balanced diet and to get adequate amounts of physical activity so that their bodies can perform in the wonderful way they were designed to.

Notes

Introduction: The Sugar Disease

1. Lee J. Sanders, "From Thebes to Toronto and the 21st Century: An Incredible Journey," *Diabetes Spectrum*, vol. 15, no. 1, 2002, p. 57.
2. Quoted in Miranda Hitti, "No End in Sight to Rapid Rise in Diabetes," *WebMD Medical News*, October 26, 2005. http://diabetes.webmd.com/news/20051026/no-end-in-sight-to-rapid-rise-in-diabetes.
3. Quoted in Richard Perez-Pena, "Diabetic Brothers Beat Odds with Grit and Luck," *New York Times*, February 5, 2006. www.nytimes.com/2006/02/05/nyregion/05diabetes.html.
4. Quoted in Sheri Colberg, *50 Secrets of the Longest Living People with Diabetes*. New York: Marlowe/Da Capo, 2007; excerpted in *Diabetes in Control.com Newsletter*, no. 391, November 21, 2007. www.diabetesincontrol.com/results.php?storyarticle=5300.
5. Quoted in Colberg, *50 Secrets*.

Chapter One: What Is Diabetes?

6. Quoted in Greg Critser, *Fat Land: How Americans Became the Fattest People in the World*. New York: Mariner, 2004. www.npr.org/templates/story/story.php?storyId=1763161.
7. Richard H. Carmona, prepared remarks delivered at American Enterprise Institute Obesity Conference, June 10, 2003. www.surgeongeneral.gov/news/speeches/obesity061003.htm.
8. Carmona, prepared remarks.
9. Richard H. Carmona, telephone interview by author, April 19, 2004.
10. Quoted in Daniel Trecroci, "Mark Consuelos Encourages Type 2s and Their Loved Ones to Take 'Diabetes Freedom'

Pledge," *Diabetes Health*, November 1, 2005. www.diabetes health.com/read/2005/11/01/4445.html.

11. Becky Allen, "The Banana Pudding Incident," unpublished.

12. Quoted in Mindy Brandenstein, telephone interview with author, May 5, 2008.

13. Mindy Brandenstein, telephone interview.

14. Alyssa Brandenstein, telephone interview with author, May 5, 2008.

Chapter Two: Diagnosis and Drug Treatment

15. Quoted in Linda von Wartburg, "Type 1 Pop Star, Nick Jonas Tells His Story," April 26, 2007. www.diabeteshealth .com/read/2007/04/26/5150.html.

16. Quoted in Wartburg, "Type 1 Pop Star, Nick Jonas Tells His Story."

Chapter Three: Managing Diabetes

17. Sheri Colberg, telephone interview with author, May 29, 2008.

18. Colberg, telephone interview.

19. Colberg, telephone interview.

Chapter Four: Living Well with Diabetes

20. Quoted in Anita Manning, "Diabetes Is No Obstacle to a Long, Healthy Life," *USA Today*, November 14, 2007. www .usatoday.com/news/health/2007-11-14-diabetes-book_ N.htm.

21. Quoted in Manning, "Diabetes Is No Obstacle."

22. Colberg, telephone interview.

23. Linda Koehler, telephone interview with author, June 12, 2008.

24. Koehler, telephone interview.

25. Koehler, telephone interview.

26. Koehler, telephone interview.

27. Koehler, telephone interview.

28. Koehler, telephone interview.

29. Robert Mandell, telephone interview with author, June 14, 2008.

30. Mandell, telephone interview.

31. Mandell, telephone interview.

32. Mandell, telephone interview.

33. Mandell, telephone interview.

34. Quoted in David Templeton, "Winning Life's Pageant and Living Well with Diabetes," *Pittsburgh Post-Gazette*, October 25, 2006. www.post-gazette.com/pg/06298/732550-114.stm.

35. Quoted in Templeton, "Winning Life's Pageant."

36. Quoted in Michael Silver, "Cutler Adjusting to Life with Diabetes," Yahoo! Sports, May 16, 2008. http://sports.yahoo.com/nfl/news?slug=ms-thegameface051608&prov=yhoo&type=lgns.

37. Quoted in Bill Williamson, "Refreshed, Cutler Ready to Tackle Disease, Football, Life," ESPN.com, May 28, 2008. http://sports.espn.go.com/nfl/columns/story?id=3416163.

Chapter Five: The Future of Diabetes

38. Quoted in University of Maryland Medical Center, "University of Maryland Medical Center Performs Its First Islet Cell Transplant to Treat Type 1 Diabetes," May 16, 2002. www.umm.edu/news/releases/first_ic_transplant.htm.

39. Quoted in University of Maryland Medical Center, "University of Maryland Medical Center Performs Its First Islet Cell Transplant."

40. Quoted in Erin Allday, "13,000 in S.F. to Discuss Diabetes Treatments," *San Francisco Chronicle*, June 6, 2008. www.sfgate.com/cgi-bin/article.cgi?f=/c/a/2008/06/06/MN9M113ARQ.DTL&tsp=1.

Glossary

autoimmune disease: A disease in which the body's immune system mistakenly attacks part of the body.

BMI: Body Mass Index, a measure of body fat based on height and weight that applies to both adult men and women. The calculation for a person's BMI is body weight divided by height (in inches, squared). A BMI of 25–30 is considered overweight, and 30 and higher is obese.

cholesterol: A fatlike substance made by the body and found naturally in foods such as beef, eggs, and dairy products.

diabetic ketoacidosis: A dangerous medical condition in which ketones build up in the blood, which happens when the body is severely low in insulin. This occurs most often in people with type 1 diabetes.

gland: A bodily organ that produces chemical substances for use in the body. One example is the pancreas, which produces insulin.

glucagon: A hormone created in the pancreas that helps glycogen in the liver to break down to glucose.

glycogen: A substance stored in the body as carbohydrates.

hemoglobin: A red protein that carries oxygen in the blood of animals with backbones.

hyperglycemic: Too much glucose in the bloodstream.

hypoglycemic: Too little glucose in the bloodstream.

ketone: A compound produced when the body uses fats for energy. If they build up too high, the result can be diabetic ketoacidosis.

neuropathy: A disease or dysfunction of the nerves outside the brain and spinal cord that makes part of the body weak or numb.

obesity: Having a high amount of body fat, making the person more than 20 percent overweight.

psyche: The human mind, soul, or spirit.

saturated fat: Fats often from animal sources that are considered to be less healthy.

trans fat: Solid fats created from oils by adding hydrogen, as in margarine. Considered to be the most unhealthy fat.

unsaturated fat: A fat that is liquid at room temperature, such as vegetable oils. Considered to be the healthiest fats.

Organizations to Contact

American Association of Diabetes Educators (AADE)
200 W. Madison Ave., Suite 800
Chicago, IL 60606
phone: (800) 338-3633 or (312) 424-2426
e-mail: aade@aadenet.org
Web site: www.diabeteseducator.org or www.aadenet.org

AADE is a multidisciplinary organization of more than ten thousand health professionals dedicated to advocating quality diabetes education and care.

American Diabetes Organization
1701 N. Beauregard St.
Alexandria, VA 22311
phone: (800) 342-2383
e-mail: askada@diabetes.org
Web site: www.diabetes.org

The American Diabetes Association is the nation's leading non-profit health organization providing diabetes research, information, and advocacy. Founded in 1940, the American Diabetes Association conducts programs in all fifty states and the District of Columbia, reaching hundreds of communities. The mission of the association is to prevent and cure diabetes and to improve the lives of all people affected by diabetes.

American Dietetic Association (ADA)
120 S. Riverside Plaza, Suite 2000
Chicago, IL 60606–6995
phone: (800) 877-1600 or (800) 877-0877
e-mail: knowledge@eatright.org
Web site: www.eatright.org

The mission of the ADA is to promote optimal nutrition and well-being for all people by advocating for its members.

Children with Diabetes
5689 Chancery Pl.
Hamilton, OH 45011
Web site: www.childrenwithdiabetes.com

The Children with Diabetes Web site is a leading destination on the Internet for families dealing with diabetes, a Web resource for parents of children with type 1 diabetes, and is dedicated to helping one find the information and support one needs and in caring for a child with diabetes.

Diabetes Exercise and Sports Association (DESA)
8001 Montcastle Dr.
Nashville, TN 37221
phone: (800) 898-4322
fax: (615) 673-2077
e-mail: desa@diabetes-exercise.org
Web site: www.diabetes-exercise.org

DESA exists to enhance the quality of life for people with diabetes through exercise and physical fitness.

Diabetes Hands Foundation
PO Box 61074
Palo Alto, CA 94306
Web site: http://diabeteshandsfoundation.org

A social networking community, in both English and Spanish, for "people touched by diabetes."

Joslin Diabetes Center
One Joslin Pl.
Boston, MA 02215
phone: (800) 567-5461
General Info and Appointments: (617) 732-2400
e-mail: diabetes@joslin.harvard.edu
Web site: www.joslin.org

Affiliated with Harvard Medical School, Joslin Diabetes Center is the world's largest diabetes research center, diabetes clinic, and provider of diabetes education.

Juvenile Diabetes Research Foundation International
120 Wall St.
New York, NY 10005-4001
phone: (800) 533-2873
fax: (212) 785-9595
e-mail: info@jdrf.org
Web site: www.jdrf.org

Driven by the needs of people with diabetes, the mission of the Juvenile Diabetes Research Foundation International is to find a cure for diabetes and its complications through the support of research. It works to accomplish this by finding and funding the best and most relevant research to help achieve a cure for this devastating disease through restoration of normal blood sugar levels, avoidance and reversal of complications, and prevention of diabetes and its recurrence.

For Further Reading

Books

Jean Betschart-Roemer, *Type 2 Diabetes in Teens: Secrets for Success*. New York: John Wiley & Sons, 2002. This book for teens with type 2 diabetes was written to help them and their families understand the illness and how to cope with it. It has a special section of tips and suggestions for parents.

Sheri Colberg and Steven V. Edelman, *50 Secrets of the Longest Living People with Diabetes*. Cambridge, MA: Marlowe/Da Capo, December 2007. Written by two experts in the field of diabetes—and who both have the illness—this book profiles fifty people in the United States who have lived the longest with diabetes, and in so doing, offers their secrets and advice about how they did it.

Sheri Colberg and Mary Friesz, *Diabetes-Free Kids: A Take-Charge Plan for Preventing and Treating Type-2 Diabetes in Children*. London: Avery, 2005. This is the first book to offer parents of children with type 2 diabetes a plan for halting the illness with diet and exercise.

James S. Hirsch, *Cheating Destiny*. Boston: Houghton Mifflin, 2006. The author is a well-known journalist and best-selling author who has type 1 diabetes, and his brother and young son also have it. This book is a personal look at diabetes, showing how it affects Hirsch and his family, and also how it affects our society.

Katherine J. Moran, *Diabetes: The Ultimate Teen Guide*. Lanham, MD: Scarecrow, 2004. This book by a nurse and certified diabetes educator, whose daughter was diagnosed with type 1 diabetes when she was three, is an informative guide for teenagers who are managing their own diabetes. It is also valuable to their family and friends who want to know more about this illness so they can better understand it and what their loved one is going through.

Alan R. Rubin, *Diabetes for Dummies*. 2nd ed. Indianapolis, IN: Wiley, 2004. As one of the top experts on diabetes in the United States, Rubin was one of the first doctors in his field to recognize the importance of patients self-testing their blood glucose. This book gives a thorough overview of diabetes in all its forms along with treatments and excellent advice for self-management of the disease.

Gary Scheiner, *Think Like a Pancreas: A Practical Guide to Managing Diabetes with Insulin*. New York: Marlowe, 2004. From an author who has diabetes and is also an exercise physiologist and certified diabetes educator, this book offers a clear guide to managing diabetes.

Internet Sources

Alyssa Brandenstein, "Alyssa's Dream," video. http://www.you tube.com/watch?v=KCCytbpCG-g.

N.R. Kleinfield, "Diabetes and Its Toll Quietly Emerge as a Crisis," *New York Times*, January 9, 2006. www.nytimes.com/2006/01/09/nyregion/nyregionspecial5/09diabetes.html?page wanted=all.

National Institutes of Health, "Fact Sheet, Type 2 Diabetes." http://64.233.167.104/search?q=cache:1gA4AihovHgJ:www.nih.gov/about/researchresultsforthepublic/Type2Diabetes.pdf+National+Institutes+health+diabetes+fact+sheet+30+years+ago&hl=en&ct=clnk&cd=1&gl=us.

Web Sites

Diabetes Mine (http://www.diabetesmine.com). This Web site and blog were created by Amy Tenderich, who was diagnosed with type 1 in 2003, as an online community where people with diabetes could go to find out information on all aspects of living with the illness.

National Diabetes Clearinghouse (http://diabetes.niddk.nih.gov/about/mission.htm). The National Diabetes Information Clearinghouse (NDIC) was created in 1978 to increase knowledge and understanding about diabetes among patients, health care providers, and the public. This site has a wealth of information about this illness (in English and Spanish) including publications, referrals to health professionals, and listings of diabetes organizations.

Index

A
A1c test, 39
African Americans, 21
Alcohol, 43
Allen, Becky, 19

B
Baker, Nicole Johnson, 68, *69*, 71
Berry, Halle, *9*
Beta cells, 15, 20
  cell lines of, 79
  tissue-engineering of, 79
Blood glucose
  monitoring, 36, *37*, 38, *59*, 75
  swings in, 57–58
Bones, 83
Brandenstein, Alyssa, 45

C
Centers for Disease Control and
  Prevention (CDC), 10, 13
Cleveland, Gerald, 10, 44
Cleveland, Robert, 10, 44
Colberg, Sheri, 44–45, 62–63
Complications, 16
  avoiding, 42–43
  prevalence of risk factors for,
  28
Consuelos, Mark, 19
Cutler, Jay, 72, *73*, 74

D
Diabetes
  diagnosis of, 34–36
  gestational, 23, 25, 34
  in history, 8

personal narratives in living
  with, 63–68, 71–72
prevalence of, 12
types of, 16, 85
See also Complications;
  Symptoms; *specific types*
Diabetes epidemic, 12–13,
  88
  reasons for, 13, 15
Diabetes Self-Management
  Education (DSME), 45
Diabetes Self-Management
  Support (DSMS), 47
Diabetic emergencies, 54, 57
Diabetic ketoacidosis, 30, 60
Diagnosis, 34–36
Digestion, 15–16
Digestive system, *18*
DNA micro array, *84*
Dull, Gladys, 10–11, 44, 51

E
Edison, Thomas, 9
Ethnic groups, , 21
Exercise, 53–54

F
Farney, Alan C., 80
Fasting plasma glucose (FPG)
  test, 34
*50 Secrets of the World's Longest
  Living People with Diabetes*
  (Colberg), 44, 62
Food and Drug Administration,
  U.S. (FDA), 41
Food pyramid, 50–51

Picture Credits

About the Author

Barbara Stahura is a writer in Tucson, Arizona. Since 1994 she has written for many publications and Web sites and has also written several books. Her first collection of personal essays, *What I Thought I Knew*, was published in September 2008. She lives with her husband, Ken Willingham, and their black cat, Goldie.